essentials

Chapter 11:
Reorganizing
American Businesses

ASPEN PUBLISHERS

essentials

Chapter 11:
Reorganizing
American Businesses

Elizabeth Warren
Leo Gottlieb Professor of Law
Harvard Law School

Wolters Kluwer
Law & Business

AUSTIN   BOSTON   CHICAGO   NEW YORK   THE NETHERLANDS

Aspen Publishers
Attn: Permissions Department
76 Ninth Avenue, 7th Floor
New York, NY 10011-5201

To contact Customer Care, e-mail customer.care@aspenpublishers.com, call 1-800-234-1660, fax 1-800-901-9075, or mail correspondence to:

Aspen Publishers
Attn: Order Department
PO Box 990
Frederick, MD 21705

Printed in the United States of America.

1 2 3 4 5 6 7 8 9 0

ISBN 978-0-7355-7654-4

Library of Congress Cataloging-in-Publication Data

Warren, Elizabeth.
   Chapter 11 : reorganizing American businesses / Elizabeth Warren.
     p. cm.
   ISBN 978-0-7355-7654-4 (alk. paper)
1. Corporate reorganization — United States. 2. Bankruptcy — United States.
I. Title.
   KF1544.W37 2008
   346.73'06626 — dc22

                                          2008030833

About Wolters Kluwer Law & Business

Wolters Kluwer Law & Business is a leading provider of research information and workflow solutions in key specialty areas. The strengths of the individual brands of Aspen Publishers, CCH, Kluwer Law International and Loislaw are aligned within Wolters Kluwer Law & Business to provide comprehensive, in-depth solutions and expert-authored content for the legal, professional and education markets.

CCH was founded in 1913 and has served more than four generations of business professionals and their clients. The CCH products in the Wolters Kluwer Law & Business group are highly regarded electronic and print resources for legal, securities, antitrust and trade regulation, government contracting, banking, pension, payroll, employment and labor, and healthcare reimbursement and compliance professionals.

Aspen Publishers is a leading information provider for attorneys, business professionals and law students. Written by preeminent authorities, Aspen products offer analytical and practical information in a range of specialty practice areas from securities law and intellectual property to mergers and acquisitions and pension/benefits. Aspen's trusted legal education resources provide professors and students with high-quality, up-to-date and effective resources for successful instruction and study in all areas of the law.

Kluwer Law International supplies the global business community with comprehensive English-language international legal information. Legal practitioners, corporate counsel and business executives around the world rely on the Kluwer Law International journals, loose-leafs, books and electronic products for authoritative information in many areas of international legal practice.

Loislaw is a premier provider of digitized legal content to small law firm practitioners of various specializations. Loislaw provides attorneys with the ability to quickly and efficiently find the necessary legal information they need, when and where they need it, by facilitating access to primary law as well as state-specific law, records, forms and treatises.

Wolters Kluwer Law & Business, a unit of Wolters Kluwer, is headquartered in New York and Riverwoods, Illinois. Wolters Kluwer is a leading multinational publisher and information services company.

This book is dedicated to
Harvey Miller and Ron Trost,
who have tried to teach me
how the Chapter 11 system really works

Table of Contents

CHAPTER 3
Operating the Business   53

CHAPTER 4
Reshaping the Business   75

CHAPTER 5

Confirming the Chapter 11 Plan   133

CHAPTER 6

Jurisdiction, Procedure, and Transnational Cases   171

Preface

The ambition of the Chapter 11 system is enormous. Failing businesses can file a petition in bankruptcy, give themselves some breathing room, and take a final chance to save their businesses. Large or small, desperately sliding into collapse or merely in serious trouble, a company can attempt to reorganize or, if necessary, can arrange a more orderly burial. This book is about that system.

A book of this scope is the product of more than a single author. Harvey Miller and J. Ronald Trost, to whom this book is dedicated, have spent years trying to teach me about Chapter 11, helping me see both its beauty and its burdens. Ken Klee and Rich Levin have also enriched my understanding of the structure and the operation of the system, teasing me with hard problems and making it abundantly clear when they thought I had something wrong. My long-time co-author Jay Westbrook has shared the wisdom of his years in practice and his continuing study of Chapter 11 both in the U.S. and abroad. Along with Jay, Katherine Porter and Edward Janger offered many helpful ideas about the manuscript. Andrew Dawson made a very careful final review, recommending several improvements. I am grateful to them all for their help.

This is a small book that tours a large system, guided on the one hand by the statutory structure and on the other by how the system operates in practice. The book sacrifices coverage of every possible twist in favor of a more coherent overview that exposes some of the tensions, the contradictions, and the genius that comprise Chapter 11. Whatever else may be learned from this book, I hope these pages give a sense of just how interesting the world of business failure and rebirth can be.

Elizabeth Warren
Cambridge, Massachusetts
July 2008

essentials

Chapter 11:
Reorganizing
American Businesses

⤳ 1 ⤳

Success, Failure, and Success Again

Businesses fail.

Sometimes they collapse in a loud crash. Sometimes they drift downward, like a balloon with a slow leak. But fast or slow, noisy or quiet, businesses that were once fueled by optimism may someday face their demise. In a free-market economy, the possibility of failure is as ever-present as the hope for success, creating the shadow that businesses ignore at their peril.

The law of business bankruptcy is the organized effort to deal with businesses in trouble. For some, a bankruptcy will be like a funeral and the subsequent reading of the will; the bankruptcy judge will preside over the demise of the company and the division of the property. For others, however, the analogy is better located earlier in time. The struggling business is in the hospital, hoping to survive but facing the real possibility of imminent death.

In this short book, we will take the aerial view of business bankruptcy. This is the fast tour, an overview that connects the main pieces and gives a sense of how the system runs. We will deal with some important ideas, but we will also take time to sample the empirical data that give a sense of the operational realities.

The centerpiece of this discussion will be on business reorganization — the internationally famous Chapter 11 of the United States Bankruptcy Code. Like success and failure, liquidation and reorganization are opposing forces. It is not possible to understand one without the other. But the remarkable feature of this portion of the American legal system is not the efficiency with which it dismantles failing businesses. The singular success of bankruptcy law is the creation of a reorganization procedure for saving businesses that would otherwise die.

Reorganization had it roots in the railroad reorganizations of the late nineteenth century. More than a hundred years later, it had blossomed into a system that successfully reorganized United Airlines, K-Mart, Owens Corning, Macy's, Winn-Dixie, KB Toys, Trump Hotels & Casino Resorts, and a long list of giant and not-so-giant companies in every sector of the American economy. Perhaps more importantly, it is the possibility of putting a troubled business into Chapter 11 that affects every negotiation between a creditor and a late-paying business debtor. Chapter 11 shapes non-court workouts, as every party carefully considers whether it would be better off with the debtor in bankruptcy. It has even begun to shape business deals as they are put together. Before they advise their clients to sign on the dotted line, careful lawyers think about what would happen if one of the business partners collapsed into bankruptcy — who would have what priorities, what protections would be available to the client, and how to structure the deal to better protect the client in the case of an eventual bankruptcy filing. Today, the shadow of Chapter 11 is cast over all aspects of business dealings, even during the most optimistic honeymoon.

In this quick tour of business failure, of near-death and rebirth, of broken promises and new opportunities to make money, Chapter 11 will remain the central focus. The technical pieces of the law give life to the overall system. But the traps for the uninitiated and the bonuses for those who know how to exploit the system will share the spotlight as we discuss this extraordinary system.

WHO FILES?

This book will focus exclusively on the businesses that file for bankruptcy. Counting the number of filings, consumer bankruptcy is a much larger fraction of the American system. According to the Administrative Office of the United States Courts (the AO), business bankruptcies are less than 5 percent of all filings. But a single business case, such as WorldCom or Enron, may involve billions of dollars and jobs, retirement accounts, and health benefits for tens of thousands of people. The wake from such a case may rock both stock markets and local neighborhoods across the country, along with the lives of many thousands of families.

The decision to separate the treatment of business and consumer bankruptcies, however, does not imply that one is more important than the other. Instead, the division is born of the fact that bankruptcy is comprised of two different legal systems that use the same courthouse and many parts of the same statute, but that are effectively separate as a matter of both policy and practice. Because human beings cannot be terminated the way corporate entities can, consumer bankruptcy is far more oriented toward economic rehabilitation of the debtor. There is little reason to continue the life of a business that cannot turn a profit, but we have not yet reached the day when we would say the same about a family.

While the ends of the spectrum are clear, the business/consumer distinction requires some line drawing in the middle. Entrepreneurs, consultants, and skilled tradespeople may run their own businesses, which puts them squarely in line for a personal bankruptcy if their business operations fail. For decades, the AO classified these failures as "business cases." Over time, however, the designation as a "business" bankruptcy mutated, and "business cases" have increasingly come to mean the bankruptcy of a legal entity, such as a corporation or a partnership.[1] About 90 percent of the Chapter 11 filers are legal fictions — mostly corporations, with a few LLCs and partnerships thrown in.[2] For this book, the corporate debtor is the prototype, although we will occasionally venture into the territory of the much smaller sole proprietorship.

WHAT DOES IT MEAN TO REORGANIZE?

"Reorganization" refers to a change in the debt obligations of the business. A company's long-term bonds that were to be paid in five years at 12 percent interest, for example, may be rewritten as longer-term bonds that will be paid in eight years at 8 percent interest. The mortgage on a business's equipment may be written down from $2 million to $1.5 million to reflect the true value of the collateral. The unsecured debt, such as what is owed to suppliers and utilities, may receive the proverbial ten-cents-on-the-dollar on their accounts. Even the owners of the business will be affected; they may be wiped out, walking away with little or no ownership interest in the reorganized company. In short, reorganization is about how to spread around the pain for a business that cannot repay its debts in full.

Some reorganizations are purely financial. That is, the business operations remain the same, while the debts are written down or eliminated and stock in the business is redistributed to the unpaid creditors. A business that has loaded up on debt may be operationally sound in the sense that revenues comfortably exceed marginal costs, but that business may have no hope of meeting a high debt service. The business has simply taken on so much debt that it threatens to sink the entire outfit.

So, for example, when Dow Corning, the company that introduced silicone-based breast implants, was overtaken with tort liability, there was no need to reorganize operations. The company had abandoned the implant business years earlier. Instead, the company needed to deal with its growing debt load. In the 1980s, Johns Manville was driven to Chapter 11 by a wave of lawsuits based on its long-defunct asbestos business, and Texaco sought bankruptcy protection when Pennzoil won a multibillion dollar lawsuit against it for interference with Pennzoil's contract to buy Getty Oil. There is no reason in such cases to shutter the business operations or even to change them. Instead, the necessary reorganization is that the rights of various stakeholders are readjusted and the overall debt burden lowered so that it does not overwhelm the company's revenues. Old equity may be wiped out, for example, while the unsecured creditors become the new stockholders. These financial reorganizations are sometimes called "balance sheet reorganizations" to reflect the fact that they take place on paper rather than by changing day-to-day operations.

Other reorganizations involve a wholesale reshuffling of the business operations. The debtor will use the breathing room provided by the protection of bankruptcy to close or to sell money-losing divisions, trim excess staff, refocus product lines, cut back on the number of company cars, and so forth. K-Mart, for example, reorganized by selling off its unprofitable stores and sprucing up the remaining locations. Steel companies reorganized by dropping peripheral lines of business and closing down their most out-of-date plants. This type of business reorganization usually produces a smaller, leaner company with a reduced debt (and interest) burden, once again able to concentrate on the core competence of the business. Many companies need both types of change. The balance sheet is overburdened with debt that the company cannot pay, and the business operations are distinctly sub-optimal. The legal rules are the same for financial reorganizations and operational reorganizations; the distinction is helpful mostly to focus the participants' attention on what problems need to be solved. The key point in either type of reorganization is that all or some large part of the business is preserved as a going concern rather than sold off one piece at a time in an old-fashioned courthouse-steps sort of sale.

Of course, there is no reason that a business could not work out a reorganization on its own, without the help of any court. Creditors can always agree to forgive debts or to rewrite the terms of a loan. In Chapter 11, however, dissenting creditors can be forced to go along with a deal worked out with a majority of creditors and according to the statutory terms. Even then, however, the effects of Chapter 11 are limited: No plan can be forced on a creditor unless it offers at least as much as that creditor would have received if the business had been liquidated. In this regard, the Chapter 11 process is quite modest. It facilitates the efficient reorganization of businesses when the parties are not able to reach agreement on their own.

A QUICK HISTORY OF BUSINESS REORGANIZATION

So long as there have been debtors, governments have struggled over what rights to give the creditors. The U.S. Constitution, a document that is noticeably short on economic pronounce-ments, reserved to the federal government the power to enact "uniform Laws on the subject of Bankruptcies throughout the United States."[3] In the following hundred years, Congress passed bankruptcy laws with broad debt forgiveness in times of panic, but it repealed those laws once times were flush. Finally, Congress passed the Bankruptcy Act of 1898, and the United States has had a bankruptcy law ever since.

The Great Depression of the 1930s brought about many social and economic changes, including the introduction of the idea of business reorganization into the legal system. Although the failing railroads of the late nineteenth century had found ways to rewrite their debt obligations using a combination of state law and strong-arm tactics, federal bankruptcy law was expanded in 1933, 1934, and 1938 formalizing a system to permit rewriting debt while a company remained in business. The 1938 Chandler Act created two separate business reorganization chapters, Chapter X for publicly traded companies and Chapter XI for "mom-and-pop" businesses. The separation was based on the insight that the elaborate procedures needed to structure the reworking of a large, complex business with a multitude of creditors was far too cumbersome for the reorganization of small, privately owned businesses.

The consequence of the division was that for forty years large public companies desperately tried to use Chapter XI rather than Chapter X. Critics of the two-part system pointed to the many failed proceedings under Chapter X, blaming its cumbersome procedures. They focused much of their wrath on the statutory requirement that the Securities and Exchange Commission (SEC) launch a full-scale investigation into the reasons for the failure of each large company. SEC practices varied, but many believed that the agency often caused significant delays during the course of the Chapter X and that those delays caused the struggling businesses to collapse completely before any reorganization plan could be tried. The possibility of delay also created leverage for the SEC, giving it the power to insist that management be replaced with a trustee to run the business or that public stockholders receive higher payments than they were otherwise due. Many observers noted the sharp contrast between the long delays of Chapter X and the relative speed of Chapter XI, which was free from SEC participation.

Another central distinction between the two chapters was the insistence in Chapter X that the management of large companies be replaced when the company filed for bankruptcy, while the management of a mom-and-pop in Chapter XI could stay on. Ultimately, the management team makes the decision whether to recommend a bankruptcy filing to the shareholders. As a result, perhaps no single feature of the Act looked more attractive to management than the opportunity to stay on to run the business that would be possible if only the business could qualify under Chapter XI.

The two-part system was not without its supporters. They argued that companies disliked Chapter X precisely because managers lost their jobs — and that the bums ought to be thrown out. They also speculated about reasons why management was eager (some said, too eager) to avoid the scrutiny of an appointed trustee who might expose earlier misdeeds. After all, these were the folks in charge as they drove the business into the ground.

Contrary to the passions of both sides in the debates, there is some evidence that management of big, publicly traded companies frequently remained in control, despite the statutory mandate of Chapter X and the pressure from the SEC to replace them.[4] A trustee was nominally in place, but the first act of the trustee was often to hire the old management team to give its advice on how to run the business and negotiate the reorganization. Even so, it is not as much fun (or as lucrative) to be the adviser to the CEO as it is to be the CEO.

The courts ruled consistently that publicly traded companies could not reorganize in Chapter XI, except under the rarest of circumstances. Nonetheless, a little like Cinderella's stepsisters trying to fit their very large feet into a tiny glass slipper, the companies kept trying. By the mid-1970s a pattern was developing. The big company would file in Chapter XI, the SEC would move for conversion to Chapter X, and the company and the SEC would negotiate about the treatment of public debt holders and shareholders. The SEC would offer to withdraw its objection to leaving the case in Chapter XI if the treatment of the stockholders and bondholders was satisfactory to the SEC. Institutional lenders, such as banks and insurance companies, saw that the process was increasingly working to their disadvantage: in effect, value was being diverted from the unpaid creditors of the business to the shareholders.

The pull between Chapter X and Chapter XI was complex enough, but a third form of business reorganization was also in place for businesses whose only asset was real estate. Ventures formed to purchase and operate an apartment complex or an office building, for example, were segregated into Chapter XII when they were in financial trouble. This chapter generally followed the model of Chapter XI, but it was specifically designed to deal with long-term real estate mortgages and other real estate finance devices.

Whether management control was the reason or something else drove the decisions, it was clear by the late 1970s that companies in financial trouble were very reluctant to enter Chapter X, where Congress said they belonged. The Bankruptcy Reform Act of 1978 was aimed directly at this reluctance, and it profoundly changed the structure of business reorganization. Known as "the Code" to distinguish it from the 1898 "Act," the new law merged Chapters X, XI, and XII into a single new chapter, today's Chapter 11. Note that the numerals were changed. Thus, a "Chapter XI" refers to a pre-1978 reorganization, while a "Chapter 11" refers to reorganizations filed after the effective date of the 1978 Code.

Under the new code, the formal distinction between a small mom-and-pop operation and a billion-dollar company was largely abolished. SEC participation was dramatically reduced. The legal presumption from the old Chapter XI that current management would stay in place was now made applicable to all cases, big and small. A big disincentive to file for bankruptcy was thereby removed, making Chapter 11 a more plausible alternative for a company — and for the management of a company — in serious financial straits. Chapter 11 was not a desired state, but more troubled companies began to weigh the benefits of reorganization.

In 2005, Congress passed a large package of amendments to the bankruptcy laws. These new laws were primarily directed toward making bankruptcy less accessible for consumers, but a package of business amendments reintroduced the small-case/big-case distinction that had been obliterated in 1978. In the 2005 amendments, Congress added a provision to treat small business cases differently from their big business cousins. This time, however, the effects of the distinction ran the other way. Instead of subjecting bigger businesses to greater scrutiny as had been done in the Chapter X/Chapter XI split, the 2005 amendments put the squeeze on small businesses. The amendments imposed new burdens on small businesses, while exempting big businesses from those new constraints. If they file for Chapter 11, these little businesses encounter increased reporting requirements, greater U.S. Trustee supervision, tighter deadlines, and more drop-dead points at which they can be forced out of Chapter 11. Structurally, the 2005 amendments added a new "small business case" definition for businesses with debts less than $2 million at the time of filing, and the new restrictions apply only to a "small business case" (11 U.S.C. §101(51D)(A)). This is the first federal statute in history to discriminate directly against small businesses by name.

Despite the hardest hammer falling on the small businesses, reorganization procedures for big businesses did not escape the 2005 amendment frenzy entirely intact. The Bankruptcy Code now gives greater leverage to suppliers and less control to management in the reorganization-plan process than in the 1978 Act. These changes have probably increased the cost of reorganization and made it somewhat more difficult to reorganize a case successfully.

WHY ENCOURAGE REORGANIZATION?

Congress has gone to great lengths to create a business reorganization system. Why not simply provide for the orderly liquidation of businesses that cannot pay their debts? What possible justification is there for permitting the continued operation of a business that is not paying its legitimate debts?

These questions are routinely asked by academics and other policy wonks, but competitors of the business who want their failing competitors to leave the marketplace (and leave the remaining customers to them) demand answers as well. Foreign businesspeople, unfamiliar with Chapter 11, sometimes ask why it exists. And those who are angered by the business's failure to meet its contractual agreements often complain loudly about a system that protects those who fail.

The short answer is that Chapter 11 preserves economic value. A piecemeal liquidation of a business — a sale on the courthouse steps of the salad spoons, mixing bowls, tables and chairs, double-door refrigerators, and leasehold of a restaurant — is likely to yield much less money than the sale of these items together as a restaurant. The same is true across a spectrum of businesses. Going concerns typically bring higher values, increasing the potential recovery for many creditors.

The downsides of a liquidation sale are many. Sales of used goods, particularly when the owner is under economic distress, often operate at sharp discounts. The original warranties have been used up, and the distressed seller will not be around to take returns if something doesn't work. There is no showroom and no free delivery. Selection and volume are limited to whatever is on hand. Someone shopping for tables and chairs, for example, might have to attend twenty or more liquidation sales to find the ones she wants to buy. Some assets may be burdened with legal restrictions that limit their value in a resale. For example, a below-market lease in a prime location may be very valuable to the ongoing business, but it may contain a no-assignment clause that makes it worthless to anyone else. Some assets, such as a permit to operate the restaurant, will become valueless if there is no restaurant. Others, such as ongoing relationships with local food suppliers or the talents of a terrific chef, will simply be lost if the creditors seize the property and sell it at auction.

The problem with losing all this value is that the business usually does not have enough money to pay all the current creditors in full. Throwing away more value hurts the creditors as a whole. So a Chapter 11 system is designed to preserve the "going concern" value—that is, to maximize the value of the business so that more value is available for the repayment of the creditors.

A reorganization system is designed to enhance the return to creditors in other ways as well. By creating a collective system, it reduces the costs of administration and the expense of each creditor's acting separately. Outside bankruptcy, each creditor watches out only for its own interests. In many businesses, that may mean there are dozens of creditors monitoring the behavior of the company, particularly as it slides into default. They must check to see if management is misbehaving, perhaps hiding assets, draining cash out of the business, prepaying themselves, or taking big risks with money that the creditors would rather see go to repayment. In addition to monitoring the debtor company, creditors need to monitor each other. Has another creditor seized prime assets or received a preferential payment? All this watching costs money. And, if a problem is discovered, trying to get the courts to do something about it will cost even more.

Creditors also face problems of coordination. It might be better for all the creditors if the debtor were sold as a going concern, but no collection law outside bankruptcy gives creditors the ability to act in concert against the business. Even when the debtor business tries to work with the creditors as a group, such restructurings are plagued by the hold-out problem. Once everyone is willing to go along with a deal and feels invested in the reorganization opportunity, one creditor will often ask for just a bit more, on the assumption that everyone else will give up a bit to hang on to the deal. The problem, of course, is that once one creditor receives a bit more, the appetites of all the other creditors are whetted and the deal quickly unravels.

Chapter 11, in contrast, is designed to stop creditor actions that pick apart the business and run up costs. It imposes new rules to govern the dissipation of assets from the business, rules that can be enforced quickly by the bankruptcy court. The law ends the hold-up actions of a handful of creditors by letting the majority bind the minority to the same pro rata treatment. It also permits creditors to act through a committee, hiring a single lawyer to represent their collective rights. When creditors spend less on lawyers' fees and when businesses spend less fighting their creditors, then the creditors recover more of their outstanding debts. The business of bankruptcy is limited to efficient debt collection, so that any rehabilitation of the business is justified only in terms of increasing the distribution to the creditors.

A number of scholars have formalized the model of creditor-protection, arguing that this is the exclusive rationale for bankruptcy. Professors Thomas Jackson and Douglas Baird advance the "creditor's bargain heuristic" to test whether a certain provision should or should not be a part of the bankruptcy scheme.[5] As they see it, bankruptcy rights should be no more — and no less — than the rights the creditors would have bargained for as a group pre-bankruptcy, if they had taken the time to do so.[6]

For others, however, a principal attraction of Chapter 11 is not just its efficiency for creditors, but the way it protects other parties who would suffer more from a liquidation.[7] For example, when a business is liquidated, employees suddenly lose their jobs. In a perfect market, they would go to work at the same salary elsewhere, but markets are rarely so perfect. Often their skill set is specific to the employer, or the next employer who could use those skills is located far away and a move would involve selling a home, uprooting children, and dealing with a spouse's job. If the employer is a big one, closing the business will disrupt the ordinary supply and demand of labor, depressing wages and making jobs even harder to find. Even if other employment is available, search costs are real.

Similarly, local taxing authorities lose out when a business closes. Tax revenues that would have been collected are lost. Property values may decline in a specific area or throughout the region. If many employees are fired, the fall in revenues coincides with an increase in the need for social services and unemployment benefits.

The ripples can be felt elsewhere. Suppliers who counted on selling to the shuttered business may themselves fail. This has been a big issue in the auto industry, as businesses that are entirely dependent on one or two buyers of specialized car parts may themselves end up in bankruptcy if the domestic automakers are threatened. Shopping malls reflect a related phenomenon. A mall without one of its anchor department stores will see a sharp decline in traffic, sufficient in some cases to sink smaller nearby businesses that depended on the anchor store traffic for their own sales.

Economists are fond of pointing out that when a business fails, its assets can be redeployed to better uses. As other businesses expand or new businesses are born to fill the void from the failed company, there will be new opportunities for all those employees, taxing authorities, suppliers, and neighbors. But even the economists are quick to concede that local dislocations may not adhere to the theoretical model. Moreover, the theoretical model works over a long time, and people, businesses, and taxing authorities need income in the short run. Even if the market eventually smoothes out, the consequences of liquidation can produce very real externalized costs in the meantime.

Congress was particularly sensitive to the impact that business liquidations have on third parties. The modernization of Chapter 11 in the 1978 Bankruptcy Code was justified in part as a way to preserve jobs and stabilize communities by reorganizing, rather than liquidating, more businesses. After the collapse of communism, many Eastern European governments expressed intense interest in an American-style Chapter 11 system that might rehabilitate failing businesses and maintain higher employment.

Of course, the benefits of Chapter 11 must always be balanced against the burdens. Leaving inefficient businesses intact is no help to the economy or ultimately to the employees, communities, and partners who do business with them. It is important that the reorganization mechanism include provisions to weed out businesses that cannot — and should not — survive on a going-forward basis. Similarly, if the costs of reorganization are too large, then the benefits cannot justify the expense. Chapter 11 is about minimizing losses, which necessarily encompasses a review of overall costs.

DISTRIBUTIVE CONSEQUENCES OF CHAPTER 11

Cost savings is a laudable goal, but it often comes at the expense of someone or something. In the case of reorganization, giving a business a chance to survive means elevating advantages for the whole group over the rights of individual creditors. In order to reap the benefits associated with reorganization rather than liquidation, some creditors may be forced to give up certain individual legal rights. A landlord, for example, may not be allowed to chain the doors of the restaurant when the business is late paying the rent, or a secured creditor may not be able to repossess a company's entire inventory when the business hasn't made its payments on time. These creditors may have the legal right outside bankruptcy to padlock the business or seize the property, but if they could exercise those rights in Chapter 11, then the business would immediately shut down and a piecemeal liquidation would follow. Therefore Chapter 11 often suspends or modifies the rights of the most powerful creditors in order to preserve value for the creditors collectively.

This brings us to the other central, theoretical feature of the bankruptcy system. A necessary corollary to the goal of preserving the value of the business is that the interests of different parties must be balanced against each other. The landlord or the secured creditor may be forced to suspend the collection rights they would have enjoyed outside bankruptcy, but that only begins the inquiry. For how long will the suspension occur? Will the landlord or the secured creditor have any rights in bankruptcy that are superior to those of the general creditors? Are all collection rights suspended, or only those that are most critical to the business's survival? Or, to put this another way, how much of the special collection rights that one creditor has by virtue of its pre-bankruptcy contracts or pre-bankruptcy collection actions will be preserved in bankruptcy, and how much will be sacrificed for the benefit of the other creditors and the social values that bankruptcy law embodies?

The distributional issue gets even more complex. Will all creditors without special non-bankruptcy rights be treated the same? Is Citibank like an employee, with both collecting the same proportion of their outstanding debts — Citibank on an $800,000,000 loan and the employee on her $800 in unpaid wages? Are taxing authorities just like inventory lenders? Should some creditors have priorities over others in the payment scheme? This is a deeply value-laden inquiry, with a strong political overlay. It is no surprise that in the priority-payment sections of the Bankruptcy Code we find special rules for family farmers and employees.

It is not enough to show that Chapter 11 preserves value in the aggregate. It is also necessary to review the benefits for the whole group against the costs for any particular individual.

By overriding non-bankruptcy law to produce more value for the creditors, bankruptcy law must also wrestle with relative rights of different creditors to demand repayments and to reap the benefits of business reorganization. In effect, bankruptcy is a constant struggle involving both allocative efficiency (eliminating waste and raising total collective value) and distributive justice (distributing the value of a reorganized business among all the stakeholders according to normative principles).

DOES CHAPTER 11 WORK?

Professors Bris, Welch, and Zho say the data back up the claim that reorganization preserves value far better than liquidation. In their study of confirmed plans, they conclude that, "the average Chapter 11 case retains value 78 percent better than the average Chapter 7 [liquidation] case."[8] In short, reorganization works.

Part of the trick in this analysis, however, is that the data are drawn only from confirmed plans of reorganization. If few businesses can confirm a plan of reorganization after filing for bankruptcy, then the promise of Chapter 11 would be largely illusory. The conventional wisdom for plan confirmation rates was established in the 1980s by a report issued by the Administrative Office of the U.S. Courts (AO), estimating a 17 percent confirmation rate for all Chapter 11 filings.[9] This was lower than the 33 percent estimated by the Brookings Institution in the 1960s under the predecessor Chapter XI bankruptcy system,[10] and the AO report helped reinforce the view that the post-1978 Bankruptcy Code's Chapter 11 plan was beset by problems.[11] Thus the conventional wisdom for plan confirmation rates under the modern regime has been a dismal one in six.

More recent data from the Business Bankruptcy Project, a project my co-author Professor Jay Westbrook and I have worked on for more than a decade. Our recent study involving Chapter 11 cases filed in 1994 and 2002 suggests a much higher confirmation rate. We discovered that about one in every three businesses that file for Chapter 11 eventually confirms a plan of reorganization.[12] This is good news, but it nonetheless indicates that failures outnumber successes by two to one.

If, however, Chapter 11 is looked at as a system designed for two functions — to sort losers from winners *and* to provide the time and space for reorganization of the winners — then the vision of Chapter 11 brightens considerably. Many businesses arrive at the bankruptcy courthouse dead-on-arrival, never able to marshal the resources needed to propose a plan of reorganization — and these businesses *shouldn't* confirm a plan. But in cases in which a debtor still has some resources and makes a serious effort at reorganization, as measured by the debtor's filing a plan of reorganization, the success rate swells to more than 70 percent.[13]

For some, a system in which three of every ten of all those that file a plan of reorganization end up failing will be deemed a high-loss system. But for those who measure it in the context of trying to save deeply troubled businesses that are otherwise destined for likely obliteration, a 70 percent confirmation rate looks like a glass very full.

It is always important to know what price is paid for the apparent successes. Here the empirical data also offer some important insights. Considering the complexity of the task, the Chapter 11 system operates with surprising rapidity. One-third of all the cases are resolved in the first six months after filing, and two-thirds have been completed within a year.[14] The other side of Chapter 11 — sorting the wheat from the chaff — also seems to be working. Failures are pushed out most quickly, with 40 percent of the doomed cases gone in six months and three-quarters gone within a year of filing. Success takes longer, but presumably it is worth waiting for. We also note that this good news about the efficiency of Chapter 11 preceded congressional efforts to "improve" the system in 2005.

We have data on confirmation rates, but confirming a plan of reorganization is not precisely the same as capturing all the benefits of a successful reorganization. Success is a relative term. Some businesses will confirm a plan of reorganization, but the newly slimmed down business has laid off a portion of its workforce and shuttered various operations. Others will be out of business within months or years after confirmation. Indeed, some Chapter 11 cases specifically design a plan that involves the sale of the business.

The complications run both ways. The failed cases — those that did not confirm reorganization plans — may have exited the system because they worked out their problems with their creditors and found a way to pay, rendering a reorganization plan unnecessary. Confirmation rates are important, as is time to confirmation, but it will never capture the full scope of the relative success and failure of Chapter 11.

There are other approaches to measuring relative success. Determining the direct costs of a Chapter 11 is a useful, but staggeringly complex operation. There are lawyers' fees, accountants' fees, and appraisers' fees. There are creditors who must deal with accelerated debts, claim forms, and demands for repayment of earlier transactions. There is the time that management spends on bankruptcy issues rather than operating the business. There are customers who turn away from a business in Chapter 11 and excellent employees who abandon the ship. There are, in effect, the direct costs of Chapter 11, including attorneys' fees, and the indirect costs, including lost value in the company.

Several researchers have looked at direct costs in the reorganization of the largest Chapter 11 cases. Professor Lynn M. LoPucki and Joseph W. Doherty examined data collected from all of the largest cases since the Bankruptcy Code went into effect in 1980, finding that the average ratio of fees and expenses to assets was 2.2 percent.[15] In other words, for a business with about $100 million in assets, a reorganization is likely to cost about $2,200,000 in legal fees. Professor Stephen Lubben looked at a somewhat different sample of large cases and concluded that direct costs in large reorganizations are approximately 2 percent of firm assets.[16] Similarly, Professor Brian Betker finds a ratio of direct costs to assets of 3.9 percent for 75 big Chapter 11 cases.[17] While these percentages seem small, the absolute values can be quite high. In Enron, for example, professional fees exceeded a billion dollars. Wow.

But the studies show significant scale effects in fees, with the percentage costs greatly (and inversely) dependent on the size of the business. Unlike the researchers who concentrated on the largest Chapter 11 cases, which comprise only a tiny fraction of all the business cases filed in a given year, Professors Stephen Ferris and Robert Lawless conducted several studies of routine business cases, which are typically much smaller. They found costs that were proportionately much higher, about 8.66 percent of all assets in one study and about 17.6 percent in another.[18] These data suggest that Chapter 11 may entail an irreducible core of costs, even in small cases, and that these costs can consume a significant fraction of a Chapter 11 payout.

To add to the complications of analyzing the costs of Chapter 11, it is important to consider the alternatives. Is a Chapter 11 reorganization expensive? Compared to what? Undoubtedly, it is less expensive for a debtor to succeed in business than to reorganize in Chapter 11, but that option is usually lost by the time parties are brushing up on their understanding of rules of bankruptcy. What about an out-of-court workout or a complete financial restructuring outside bankruptcy? Professor Stuart Gilson finds that when reorganizations in bankruptcy and out of bankruptcy are compared for large, publicly traded companies, Chapter 11 is the cheaper alternative.[19]

The data give a bare outline of some features of Chapter 11 cases, but the most far-reaching effects of Chapter 11 may not be among the cases that file for bankruptcy protection. Instead, its deepest effects may be felt in the many private negotiations that occur whenever someone is struggling to meet a business obligation. Workouts occur in the shadow of bankruptcy, with each party keeping a careful eye on what would be gained and what would be lost if the business were pushed into Chapter 11. As such, Chapter 11 sets the rules for negotiation of many business deals, even if those deals never end up in a court filing.

FINAL NOTES

Throughout this book, the twin themes of preserving value and allocating value among competing parties will appear and reappear. The Chapter 11 story will be told in sequence in the next four chapters: initiating a proceeding, stabilizing business operations, reshaping the business structure, and confirming a plan of reorganization. In each area, the two themes will provide the framework for evaluating the effectiveness of the Chapter 11 structure.

~ 2 ~

Getting Started

THE FILING DECISION

The Bankruptcy Code provides surface neutrality: Either debtors or creditors can initiate a bankruptcy proceeding (11 U.S.C. §303). In point of fact, however, involuntary bankruptcy petitions (filed by the creditors) are so rare that the Administrative Office of the United States Courts quit publishing the data on the number of involuntary cases nearly twenty years ago.[1] Occasionally a creditor may see a reason to force a debtor into bankruptcy, particularly in cases when the creditor suspects fraud or otherwise wants a court to intervene. More often, however, creditors can simply make continuing operations impossible, seizing property or initiating crippling lawsuits, thereby forcing a Chapter 11 filing that is voluntary in name, even if the dynamics suggest otherwise.

Nearly all Chapter 11 reorganization cases are initiated by the debtor, an act termed a "voluntary petition." Filing a bankruptcy petition is an extraordinary move for a business, and corporations need a vote of their board of directors to authorize the business to act. The mechanical process is straightforward. With the help of counsel, the business executives fill out detailed forms, including a petition to the court for bankruptcy relief and schedules that list all the business's income, assets, and liabilities. The petition and accompanying schedules are filed with the Clerk of the Bankruptcy Court, along with a filing fee. Petitions are nearly always filed electronically, with the time recorded to the minute. Paper petitions are also date and time stamped because a number of bankruptcy rules will turn on the exact timing of certain events, including the timing of the bankruptcy petitions. With just this filing — with no court hearings and no affidavits from other people, with no proof about the red ink on the balance sheet or the measures already taken to pay creditors — the bankruptcy petition is accepted by the clerk, and the business is officially bankrupt.

For some, the technical ease of filing for bankruptcy comes as a bit of a shock. Disputes over insolvency and litigation over eligibility to file for bankruptcy are largely absent from the U.S. system. That is a deliberate policy choice, made on the assumption that very few businesses would choose to file bankruptcy unless they needed it. Wasting time and resources to litigate eligibility for bankruptcy is likely to doom the last fragile hope for reorganization. The Code permits litigation in a contested involuntary bankruptcy cases and for the rare case in which the creditors believe they can show that the bankruptcy filing was made in bad faith, but those cases are rare exceptions. In the overwhelming majority of cases, the decision by those who run the troubled business will determine whether the company does or does not become a bankruptcy statistic.

In making the decision whether to seek the protection of Chapter 11, a corporate board may consider a number of factors. The opportunity to save a distressed business is the central attraction for most, and much of the remainder of this book focuses on how Chapter 11 gives an otherwise-dying business a last chance to survive.

But Chapter 11 is not a completely safe haven for troubled businesses, and decision makers often must weigh a number of costs that will burden this decision. In addition to the substantial costs associated with lawyers and accounts, a

Chapter 11 filing will change the basic operation of the business. The filing forms themselves require substantial disclosure of intimate details of the business's operations and current status — information that will become publicly available at the moment of filing. (Bankruptcy records are now accessible online.) In addition to the information required at the moment of filing, a bankruptcy court may require the officers and directors of the business to reveal more information as the case unfolds. Even communications between corporate employees and corporate attorneys that would ordinarily be protected by attorney-client privilege may be forcibly disclosed in the course of a bankruptcy case. A business with any secrets to keep must understand that one price to pay for filing is complete and full disclosure of everything from business operations to hiring practices to anything else that may bear on the business's success or failure. In Chapter 11, the debtor's past hangs out in full view of the world.

A board may also consider the very real possibility that it will lose control of the business after a Chapter 11 filing. Creditors' immediate collection rights are sharply limited in bankruptcy, but the creditors' collective ability to direct the fate of the business increases dramatically. In the eyes of the law, the bankrupt business is now to be run for the benefit of the creditors; shareholders are to be considered only in the unlikely event that the creditors will be paid in full. If assets and income projections are not enough to pay off the creditors, the current shareholders may be stripped of their ownership stake. Indeed, despite filing in Chapter 11, the business may be sold intact to third parties or it may be liquidated piecemeal. At the instant of filing, no one knows the eventual outcome of the case.

Although most would deny it, managers are surely aware of the fact that a Chapter 11 filing is not likely to enhance their own job security — or their resumes when they look for other work. In their empirical study of large business bankruptcies,

Professors Lynn LoPucki and William Whitford note that the price that current management of a large publicly held company often pays for crashing a business into Chapter 11 is that they must give up management control and leave the company.[2] It is important to note, however, that these studies were of large corporations, often those with powerful institutional investors, sometimes strong unions, and sophisticated creditors with substantial resources. In an earlier study of smaller, closely held companies, LoPucki found that if the small company survived the Chapter 11 filing, the owner-managers virtually never lost control.[3]

Whether the company files at the tip of a sword — forced by angry creditors who are shutting down the business operations — or files on its own initiative after devising a clever strategy to enhance the business's survival, Chapter 11 is a momentous event in the life of any business. A life-or-death struggle is underway, and a new set of legal rules laid out in Chapter 11 will govern the strategies and outcome.

THE BANKRUPTCY ESTATE

In law, the death of a live human being is automatically accompanied by the creation of an estate to be administered by certain legal rules specific to decedent's estate. The filing of a voluntary bankruptcy petition creates a similar legal separation. At the instant a company files a bankruptcy petition, all property that had belonged to the company is immediately transferred by operation of law to a new entity: the bankruptcy estate (11 U.S.C. §541). At that same instant, also by operation of law, the estate comes under the full protection of federal bankruptcy law (11 U.S.C. §362(a)). From that moment on, no one can commence or continue any act to collect any obligation owed by the pre-bankruptcy debtor (11 U.S.C. §362(a)). All claims against the pre-bankruptcy debtor become claims against the bankruptcy estate for resolution in the bankruptcy process.

The heart of the bankruptcy system is this sharp cleavage separating the debtor's pre-filing past and the estate's post-filing future. From that moment forward, both the benefits and the burdens of Chapter 11 will belong to the new estate, which will bear the responsibility of maximizing value for the creditors collectively.

THE AUTOMATIC STAY

Critical to the operation of the bankruptcy system is its impo-sition of an automatic stay against all attempts to collect from the debtor. The automatic stay is drafted in the broadest terms possible. The Code has multiple ways to tell creditors to stop their collection efforts. The stay operates against any attempt to begin or to continue any legal proceedings against the debtor (11 U.S.C. §362(a)(1)). It operates against the enforcement of any judgment already obtained (11 U.S.C. §362(a)(2)). It oper-ates against any attempt to obtain possession or control of property of the estate (11 U.S.C. §362(a)(3)). It operates against any attempt to create, perfect, or enforce a pre-petition lien (11 U.S.C. §362(a)(4),(5)). It operates against any setoff of a pre-petition debt (11 U.S.C. §362(a)(7)). It stops any proceedings before the U.S. Tax Court (11 U.S.C. §362(a)(8)). Perhaps the clearest statement of the overall intent of the automatic stay is that filing a bankruptcy petition operates as a stay against "any act to collect, assess, or recover a claim against the debtor that arose before the commencement of the case under this title" (11 U.S.C. §362(a)(6)).

In order to make the protection of the automatic stay as complete as possible, the stay operates as a prohibition against "all entities" — including the sheriff, the U.S. marshal, the col-lection agency, and the creditor who is owed the money.

Moreover, the automatic stay protects the business and all its property. The stay applies to actions against the debtor (11 U.S.C. §362(a)(1), (2), (6), (7), (8)), against property of the estate (11 U.S.C. §362(a)(2), (3), (4)), and against property of the debtor (11 U.S.C. §362(a)(5)).

Not every entity that is owed an obligation by a bankrupt debtor will think of itself as a creditor. Indeed, for many parties there may be a dispute over whether a debt is owed at all. Nonetheless, the automatic stay applies to all claims against the estate, including claims that are disputed, claims that are contingent, and claims that are unliquidated (11 U.S.C. §101(5)). So, for example, if a business guarantees a debt for another company and that other company is performing, the guaranty is a claim—a claim that is contingent on the other company's failure to pay. If the business dumped toxic waste, its obligation to clean it up might be clear, but the amount due might still be the subject of a dispute. Such a debt would be unliquidated. Thus, the attempt to continue a lawsuit in order to show that a debt is due or to determine the amount that is owed is part of an attempt to collect a debt, and it stops dead in its tracks. Even creditors asking for equitable remedies such as specific performance or an injunction rather than money payments must cease their efforts. Both requests for remedies and requests for payments are collection attempts under the Code, and both must halt (11 U.S.C. §101(5)).

Creditors that violate the stay are subject to sanctions, including fines and civil imprisonment until they comply with the court's order. (Sanctions are discussed in more detail in the section on court jurisdiction.) Moreover, collection actions in violation of the automatic stay are generally treated as having no effect. The Code requires creditor compliance even if the creditor has not received a formal notice of the filing (11 U.S.C. §362). A violation is a violation; knowledge of the filing is relevant only to the question of willfulness and the scope of an appropriate remedy. Violations of the automatic stay can result in contempt citations. The Code specifically provides for remedies when live human being debtors are injured by a violation of the automatic stay; they may collect costs and attorneys' fees and, in cases involving willful violations, punitive damages (11 U.S.C. §362(k)). Corporate debtors that have been injured rely on the bankruptcy courts' general equitable powers for enforcement.

In real terms, once a petition is filed, creditors may not continue to ask for payment of pre-petition obligations. They cannot make calls or send bills to collect. They cannot sell the debtor's property at a private sale or permit the sheriff to sell the property at a judicial sale. They cannot repossess property, and they cannot retain property they repossessed earlier. They cannot take a security interest, perfect a lien, or set off a debt. They cannot initiate a lawsuit against the debtor or continue a lawsuit in progress. Any post-filing enforcement of any obligations against the debtor must be channeled through the bankruptcy court. The automatic stay freezes creditor action.

In contrast, the bankrupt business may continue to operate, to use collateral, to spend money, and so on, subject to the restrictions discussed in the next chapter. It may even continue to pursue its own lawsuits against others. But actions against the business cease, creating a markedly different operating environment for the post-filing business, free from unchecked creditor activity.

Who Benefits from the Stay

Collection actions are not always confined to a single party. A business filing for bankruptcy may be just one of the defendants in a pending lawsuit. For example, a creditor may sue a tortfeasor and its insurance company, an obligor and its guarantor, a corporation and its directors, or a partnership and its individual partners. It is not uncommon for one party to file for bankruptcy while its co-defendant does not. In such instances, the non-bankrupt party may ask for a stay of collection activities against it while the bankruptcy proceeds and the bankrupt debtor makes efforts to pay some portion of the joint obligation.

Nothing in Section 362 extends the stay beyond the named debtor, property of the debtor, and property of the estate. Nonetheless, the Code gives the bankruptcy court a general equitable power to effectuate its decisions. "The court may issue any order, process, or judgment that is necessary or appropriate to carry out the provisions of this title" (11 U.S.C. §105(a)). To have a meaningful automatic stay against the debtor, courts have sometimes invoked this provision to extend the stay to include other parties. Typically, they have done so when collection efforts against a non-filing party would injure the estate. Such injury might occur in any number of ways. For example, a debtor might be called on to defend a suit against the CEO, thus drawing management's time and attention away from its reorganization efforts. In such situations, some courts have stayed actions against officers of the debtor corporation. Or the result of a suit against a related party might increase liability against the estate; in these cases, some courts have stayed actions against insurers or cosigners with rights of indemnification. Finally, successful collection against a party might deplete assets that the debtor could otherwise draw upon in reorganizing. Faced with this possibility, some courts have stayed actions against the individual partners of a debtor partnership when they have promised to help fund the partnership's repayment plan, but this move is controversial — a sort of bankruptcy benefit without the burden of all the bankruptcy rules regarding filing, disclosure, pro rata treatment of all creditors, and so on.

Exceptions to the Stay

Not surprisingly for a provision so broadly written, there are also some statutory exceptions to the automatic stay. But these exceptions are drafted narrowly to permit only limited activities against the estate.

The specific exceptions meet a number of different but fairly obvious objectives. Criminal proceedings against the debtor may continue (11 U.S.C. §362(b)(1)). The reason for this exception is not surprising. The Code is designed to apportion losses among creditors, not to provide a refuge from the enforcement of criminal laws. The government has an interest in enforcing criminal laws, which the drafters of the Code decided would take precedence over bankruptcy's automatic stay. At the margins when enforcement of criminal sanctions involves the payment of money, such as restitution payments for criminal activity or the prosecution of bad-check charges, the courts have struggled to separate debt collection attempts that should be stayed by a bankruptcy petition from criminal penalties that should proceed regardless of the bankruptcy. In general, the distinction the courts have settled on looks at whether the state is attempting to collect a pre-petition debt (in violation of the bankruptcy system's principles of distribution) or whether it is trying to enforce the social interests articulated in a criminal prohibition (to which the bankruptcy system explicitly defers).

A second exception permits a governmental unit to commence or to continue an action to enforce its "police or regulatory power" without violating the automatic stay (11 U.S.C. §362(b)(4)). In part, this provision supplements the power granted to the state in subsection (b)(1) dealing with criminal proceedings. But it also extends that power by allowing the state to pursue a wide range of regulatory objectives that do not involve criminal sanctions. Here is the authority for a governmental unit to continue enforcement of prohibitions on polluting, employee safety regulations, and licensing requirements even against the new bankruptcy estate. Again, however, collection functions and regulatory functions sometimes overlap. The government might, for example, seek both payment to compensate the government for its clean-up of an earlier toxic spill and a prohibition against future dumping. The regulatory exception is somewhat more narrowly drawn than the criminal action exception, providing relief from the prohibition of Section 362(a)(1) on efforts to commence or continue proceedings, but not from the other provisions of the automatic stay, which prohibit efforts to collect. Once again, the court must untangle which actions are encompassed by the stay and which are not. And again, the guiding principle is whether the state is attempting to collect a pre-bankruptcy obligation from the estate, in which case it will have to process that claim through the bankruptcy court, or is exercising police or regulatory powers, in which case the Code defers to the regulators.

The section on exceptions to the stay is long, but it is mostly about narrow exceptions that permit certain regulatory or ministerial functions. The government is authorized to enforce certain regulations.[4] A lender with a purchase money security interest obtained within thirty days before the bankruptcy filing can still record the security interest and it will be treated as if it had been filed just before the bankruptcy (11 U.S.C. §§362(b)(3), 547(e)(2)(A)). A creditor with a statutory lien that requires subsequent actions to perfect, such as a subcontractor on a building project, may complete its perfection after the business has filed for bankruptcy by giving notice (11 U.S.C. §§362(b)(3), 546(b)). A landlord may remove a bankrupt tenant if the nonresidential lease terminated before the filing, in effect making it clear that such eviction is not an action to collect (11 U.S.C. §362(b)(10)). A holder of a negotiable instrument may present the instrument for notice and dishonor, largely to preserve its rights under U.C.C. Articles 3 and 4 (11 U.S.C. §362(b)(11)). But in none of these cases may the creditor act to collect an outstanding debt.

A party that can claim its activities are protected by an exception to the stay may continue the activities without court approval. Such a party acts at its own peril, however.

If it is mistaken in believing that an exception applies to its activities, that party has violated the stay and it could be subject to sanctions.

Lifting the Stay

A creditor that wants to pursue a debt must ask for the permission of the bankruptcy court by filing a motion to lift or modify the automatic stay. The grounds for lifting a stay are very limited, and are available only to secured creditors. Once the secured creditor makes an appropriate motion, the court will lift the stay (1) for cause, including lack of adequate protection of a creditor's interest in property; (2) if the debtor does not have equity in property subject to a security interest and the property is not necessary to an effective reorganization; (3) in real estate cases, 90 days after filing if the debtor has neither filed a reorganization plan nor resumed monthly payments on the property; or (4) if a debtor is engaged in a fraudulent action to block a real estate foreclosure with repeated bankruptcy filings (11 U.S.C. §362(d)).

Relief from the automatic stay centers around permission for a secured creditor to repossess the collateral that is the subject of its security interest notwithstanding the stay imposed in bankruptcy. Thus, the first overtly distributional balance of the Bankruptcy Code finds expression here: Creditors with perfected security interests receive better treatment than creditors without such interests. The automatic stay bars secured creditors from repossessing collateral, but, under the circumstances described above, they can obtain permission to lift the stay or to receive payments to protect their interests. Unsecured creditors have no corresponding right.

When the court grants or denies the secured creditor the right to repossess collateral that has become property of the estate, the interests of an individual creditor are effectively balanced against the collective interests of those who are helped by survival of the estate. The balance involves both value-enhancing and distributional aspects. Often, the estate will be more valuable if the property is left in place, but the secured creditor will run a greater risk of nonpayment than if it could immediately seize the property. The Code settles on a compromise: Secured creditors have somewhat protected status. The key distributional decision is obvious. On the one hand, secured creditors are not forced to give up all their possessory and collection rights and to participate pro rata with the unsecured creditors. On the other hand, their repossession rights are cut back so that the estate can benefit from the use of the collateral.

The details of the balance show the extent to which the bankruptcy system will deviate from a principle of equality of distribution in order to protect the preferred position of some creditors. The Code instructs the court to lift the stay, permitting repossession and liquidation of a piece of the estate, if the creditor is not given "adequate protection" of its interest in the property (11 U.S.C. §362(d)(1)).

If the collateral is stable in value and unlikely to suffer either market decline or casualty loss, a court may determine that the creditor is adequately protected and the property will then be left in the estate. If, for example, the collateral is a valuable piece of machinery, fully insured and unlikely to decline in value as the estate uses it, a court will be unlikely to grant a creditor's motion to lift the stay. The court will most likely conclude that the creditor's interest is adequately protected simply by leaving the property in place.

For collateral that might decline in value, the Code provides that the estate may satisfy the adequate-protection requirement in a number of different ways and thereby retain the property. The estate may make cash payments to offset the decline in value, or it may provide additional or replacement liens on other property of the estate to offset the declines (11 U.S.C. §361(1), (2)). Alternatively, the court may fashion any other relief that will give the secured party the "indubitable equivalent" of its interest in the collateral (11 U.S.C. §361(3)). If the collateral is a production machine, for example, the court may require the debtor to maintain insurance and to make payments equal to its depreciation.

When the court permits the estate to retain possession of collateral during the bankruptcy proceeding, it determines that the creditor's interest represented by the property is unlikely to diminish. Of course, for anyone familiar with the concept of the time value of money, it is clear that the secured creditor suffers from this delay. Repossessing and liquidating the collateral immediately is obviously worth more to the creditor than repossessing and liquidating months or even years hence in the course of the Chapter 11 proceeding, even if precisely the same sale price is achieved at either date. The appropriate balance was disputed in the courts of appeals in the 1980s, but the Supreme Court resolved the issue in *In re Timbers of Inwood Forest Association*,[5] holding that "adequate protection" requires protection of the value of the collateral but does not require compensation for what the debtor lost because of the time value of money as a result of its inability to repossess. Thus a creditor could successfully lift the stay if it is owed $500,000 secured by collateral worth $400,000 if the collateral is declining in value by $10,000 each month and the debtor is making no payments to offset the loss. But if the value of the collateral is steady and the creditor's only loss is the interest it could make if it could foreclose the property and invest the cash elsewhere, the creditor is simply stuck during the bankruptcy process. The balance is clear: The secured party loses some rights (the right of immediate repossession and concomitant cash-out) to enhance the value of the estate, but it retains some rights (e.g., the right to repossess if the debtor cannot ensure adequate protection) that put it ahead of the general unsecured creditors.

A somewhat different balance is reflected in the second provision under which the creditor may get the stay lifted and repossess collateral. If the debtor has no equity in the property and the property is not necessary to an effective reorganization, the stay will be lifted and the secured creditor may repossess, liquidate immediately, and get its cash. The debtor cannot resist by showing that it can safeguard the creditor's position with adequate protection payments. Instead, if the creditor can show that the property is not essential to the business ("is not necessary to an effective reorganization") and the estate has no economic interest in the property ("debtor does not have an equity in such property"), the secured creditor prevails. So, for example, if the bankrupt business has a beautiful $10 million Rothko painting hanging in corporate headquarters, the bank with a security interest in the painting and an outstanding debt of $12 million is likely to be granted the right to seize and sell it to satisfy as much of the outstanding debt as possible. After all, the business is unlikely to be able to show that the painting is necessary for the reorganization, and the liens against the painting exceed its value, so the estate has no equity in the property, that is, has no value to protect for the benefit of the general unsecured creditors.

This provision illustrates another aspect of the balance between the individual secured creditor and the collective interests of the estate: Secured creditors' possessory rights will be impaired only if the debtor has equity in the property and the property is needed for the reorganization that will benefit the creditors collectively.

A third option to lift the automatic stay has a far more limited scope. It applies only to Single Asset Real Estate cases, or SAREs as they are called in the trade.[6] A typical example would be a corporation or partnership whose only asset is an apartment house or office building and whose only substantial debt is the mortgage on it. Such a case often amounts to a two-party struggle between the owner and the mortgage lender, with few other creditors or employees involved. When Congress created Chapter 11 in 1978, it abolished Chapter XII, which was a separate reorganization chapter for real estate cases, but it could not abolish the economic factors that make such cases quite different from the typical Chapter 11, which is a multi-party dispute.

Because such cases often involve only a single creditor, many have argued that the collective remedy of bankruptcy is not necessary. The rights of the debtor and creditor could be resolved through state law debt collection. Whether it was stirred by policy or by hard lobbying from the lending industry, Congress finally agreed to make it easier for mortgage lenders in SAREs to lift the automatic stay. If the estate fails to file a plan of reorganization or make payments equal to the mortgage payment within 90 days of filing, a mortgage lender in a SARE case can move for relief from the automatic stay. This leaves the lender free to foreclose on the property under state law rules, presumably with no real loss imposed on any other creditors because, in theory, there are no other creditors.[7]

Implications of Stay Litigation

Stay litigation often begins within days of the bankruptcy filing and quickly accelerates into a life-or-death struggle for the estate. The secured creditor, fearful of holding an interest in declining collateral that it cannot sell, wants to repossess. The estate recognizes that without the collateral the business will collapse. Stay litigation, with its heavy dependence on current and future valuation, is intensely fact-specific. Moreover, the courts are called upon to make judgments about the future valuations of both the property and the business, often being forced to decide early in the case whether the business has any hope of enhancing its value if it remains under the protection of the bankruptcy court.

If the stay is lifted too easily, the estate has no opportunity to enhance the value of the property to be distributed. Distribution to the creditors is closer to general collection law — the secured creditor takes the critical property and the other creditors line up for what little is left. If the stay is not lifted when it is appropriate, however, the value of the collateral can be dissipated as the business struggles on in a hopeless quest. Moreover, if the value of the property declines below the amount owed to the secured creditor, the injury is imposed on that creditor directly and not shared among the creditors generally, which effectively imposes a different distributional scheme from the one articulated in the Code.

Disputes over the automatic stay are among the most common in bankruptcy. The consequences of this litigation are critical, and a delay in lifting the stay can cost the secured creditor dearly. In recognition of these factors, the Code provides for accelerated treatment of stay litigation. A stay is terminated 30 days after a creditor moves for relief, unless a court has ruled that the stay shall remain in effect (11 U.S.C. §362(e)). Empirical evidence suggests, however, that stay litigation often takes much longer.[8] The same factors that make it important to have an immediate answer also make it difficult for the court to rule within such a tight schedule. Usually the parties are engaged in a monumental struggle over whether the business will continue operations. Other pressing matters, including emergency orders permitting businesses to stay in operation, are known to crowd out immediate resolution of stay litigation. The bankruptcy courts tend to be sensitive to the consequences of delaying decisions that affect the survival of the business and tend to give stay litigation a high priority. Even so, continuances are not uncommon when relief from the stay is sought in the early days of a case.

PROPERTY OF THE ESTATE

The automatic stay and the creation of the bankruptcy estate occur at the same instant. When the business files for bankruptcy, all of its legal and equitable interests in any property are transferred to the estate (11 U.S.C. §541). This transfer is automatic and unconditional. With a few exceptions discussed below, the Bankruptcy Code overrides any restrictions on transfer that would be enforceable against the business if it were not in bankruptcy.

What Is Property of the Estate?

Property of the estate encompasses the widest possible sweep of property of the business filing for bankruptcy. "All legal or equitable interests of the debtor" as of the commencement of the case are conveyed to the estate (11 U.S.C. §541(a)(1)). The debtor's interest may be full ownership, or it may be something less, such as the possessory interest of a lessee. Whatever the scope of the debtor's interests, the estate succeeds to them. Similarly, it does not matter where the property is held. Any property of the business that is in the custody of others is automatically transferred to the estate, and the custodians of such property are required to turn it over to the bankruptcy estate as soon as they learn of the bankruptcy (11 U.S.C. §§541(a)(3), 543 (a)).

Claims of a bankrupt business against others are another form of property of the estate. Warranty claims benefiting the debtor, lawsuits the debtor might pursue against others, insurance proceeds covering the debtor's losses, claims of a bankrupt debtor partnership against its general partners, and claims of a corporate debtor against its officers and directors can all be valuable. And they all become claims that belong to the bankruptcy estate (11 U.S.C. §541(a)(1)).

The estate also becomes the owner of the books and financial records of the bankrupt business (11 U.S.C. §542(e)). Attorneys, accountants, and others with information about the debtor's financial circumstances may be required to disclose such information (11 U.S.C. §542(e)).

After the bankruptcy filing, the estate may continue to grow. The estate can conduct business after filing, generating new property that becomes property of the estate (11 U.S.C. §§1108, 541(a)(7)). Property in the estate may produce more property, such as rents and proceeds, and that property, too, comes into the estate (11 U.S.C. §541(a)(6)). Life insurance, such as "key man" insurance that companies often hold to insure against the loss of a critical employee, that is paid to the company as beneficiary within 180 days of the bankruptcy filing also accrues to the estate (11 U.S.C. §541(a)(5)(C)). In addition, all post-bankruptcy income earned by corporate debtors is property of the estate, as it is earned.

In addition to everything the pre-bankruptcy debtor owned, the estate also enjoys rights to property unavailable to the debtor outside bankruptcy. For example, the estate may recover payments made to creditors during the ninety days before filing, even though the debtor itself had no right to demand back money it had paid on lawful debts (11 U.S.C. §§541(a)(3), 547(b), 550). Similarly, property may be brought into the estate through equitable subordination, setting aside fraudulent conveyances, avoiding liens, voiding preferential payments, and reversing unapproved post-petition transfers (11 U.S.C. §541(a)(3), (4)). The methods for doing this will be discussed in later chapters, but for now it is critical to see that the estate is everything that the business owned — and more.

One of the most difficult questions for courts to decide has been whether some bundle of rights needed to operate the business, often a license issued to the debtor by the government or a private agency, is property to which the bankruptcy estate succeeds. Taxicab medallions, commercial airline landing slots, liquor licenses, and seats on the stock exchange are assets of this kind. It is easy to appreciate the sorts of conflicts they create. On the one hand, the bankruptcy estate wants to claim the rights, either because it plans to use them in its reorganization effort or because they have significant economic value that the estate hopes to realize by transferring them to someone else. On the other hand, the licensing agency, anxious to retain control within its regulatory sphere, insists that the rights must either remain with the pre-bankruptcy debtor or be cancelled if there is any attempt to transfer the rights to a third party — including the estate.

Although there is no clear dividing line, the courts generally follow a principle that, if the only restriction on assignment is a contractual agreement between the parties (e.g., a no-assignment clause in a manufacturing contract), then the license can be assigned. But if the license could not be assigned outside bankruptcy for reasons other than a contractual no-assignment clause, the license is not assignable in bankruptcy.[9] This distinction would mean that personal-services contract, such as a contract to paint someone's portrait, that could not be assigned under common law cannot be assigned if the painter filed for bankruptcy. Any change in the identity of the performing party that upsets the reasonable expectations of the contracting parties is unlikely to be permitted in bankruptcy. These distinctions reappear in greater detail in the section on executory contracts in Chapter 4.

Property Excluded from the Estate

The exclusions of property from the estate of the debtor are even more narrowly drawn than are the exceptions to the automatic stay. The exclusions have little economic value for the creditors, and they might well be characterized as de minimis. The powers a debtor exercises solely for the benefit of others, for example, as trustee for a trust, do not come into the estate (11 U.S.C. §541(b)(1)). Also, the Code states that any interest of a lessee debtor under a nonresidential lease that has terminated before the bankruptcy filing is not property of the estate, thus creating a counterpart to the exception to the automatic stay for a lessor who wants to remove a debtor whose lease terminated prior to filing (11 U.S.C. §§541(b)(2), 362(b)(10)). The overarching rule is clear: If the debtor has an interest pre-bankruptcy, that interest belongs to the estate once the bankruptcy petition is filed.

Turnover of Property of the Estate

Anyone holding property of the estate will be required to hand that property (or the value of that property) back to the estate (11 U.S.C. §542(a)). Once again, this may give the estate a possessory interest even in property in which the pre-bankruptcy business had no such interest. So, for example, a creditor may have lawfully repossessed property prior to the bankruptcy filing, but the debtor's right to the collateral is not cut off until the property has been sold. (If the debtor can come up with the money, even state law will let the debtor redeem the property.) If the debtor files for bankruptcy after a repossession, the bankrupt business's interest in that property goes into the estate. Once a court issues a turnover order, the creditor must return the property, lest it run afoul of the automatic stay that protects all property of the estate, wherever it is held[10] (11 U.S.C. §§541(a), 542(a)).

CREDITORS' CLAIMS AGAINST THE ESTATE

Just as property of the debtor becomes property of the estate at filing, claims against the debtor become claims against the bankruptcy estate. The transfer of obligations from the bankrupt business to the estate works in tandem with the establishment of property of the estate and the imposition of an automatic stay, completing the separation between the pre-bankruptcy debtor and the post-filing entity, the estate.

Pre-Bankruptcy Claims

The separation of the old business from the new bankruptcy estate is evident in the claims process. Claims are divided in the first instance into pre-bankruptcy claims against the estate inherited from the debtor and post-filing claims, which are obligations of the estate itself. The implications of this distinction become clearer in the course of running the post-bankruptcy business operations and making plan payments as part of a plan of reorganization. For now, it is sufficient to note that post-filing claims are priority claims against the estate, to be paid in full before the estate may make any distributions to pre-bankruptcy unsecured creditors (11 U.S.C. §§507(a)(2), 503(b)). In other words, the estate pays its own bills first and only then distributes the remainder to the pre-bankruptcy creditors. A key function of the bankruptcy estate is to deal with the pre-bankruptcy claims against the debtor business. Once again, the Code is written in expansive language: A "claim" encompasses both rights to payment and rights to an equitable remedy that gives rise to a right to payment (11 U.S.C. §101(5)(A)(B)). An unpaid bill is a claim, as is a right to specific performance, for example, if the claim can be reduced to money damages. In the former case, money is owed, and in the latter, money damages can be awarded as an alternative remedy.

A debtor need not be in default on a claim for the claim to be dealt with in bankruptcy. A claim may be reduced to judgment or not, liquidated or unliquidated, fixed or contingent, legal or equitable, secured or unsecured (11 U.S.C. §101(5)(A)). So that all claims can be dealt with in the course of the bankruptcy, the amounts owed on all debts are accelerated. For example, a mortgage lender's claim against a bankrupt debtor is not simply for the month or two that the debtor was in arrears before filing. Instead, the lender's claim is for the entire balance (11 U.S.C. §502(b)(1)). When the exact amount of the claim is unknown, the bankruptcy courts routinely estimate the amount of the claims. A personal injury suit, for example, may not yet have a fixed value, but the court can estimate it for purposes of participation in the Chapter 11 case. If the claim is contingent or unliquidated, as, for example, when liability has not yet been established, the court will also estimate the value, taking into account the possibility that there might have been nothing due outside bankruptcy (11 U.S.C. §502(c)).

The breadth of the concept of a claim is illustrated by the 1985 Supreme Court decision in *Ohio v. Kovacs*.[11] The state had obtained a mandatory injunction under its environmental protection laws requiring Mr. Kovacs to clean up pollution he had caused while running his business. When he filed for bankruptcy, the state argued that the obligation under the environmental laws was not a "claim" for bankruptcy purposes because it was deeply entwined in government regulatory matters, and hence could not be paid pro rata and discharged. The Supreme Court disagreed, with the result that the clean-up claim was to be processed — and presumably discharged — in bankruptcy. All obligations owed by the pre-bankruptcy business become claims against the bankruptcy estate.

Generally speaking, the substantive claims of a creditor are neither enlarged nor narrowed by the bankruptcy filing. A claim that is not valid against the debtor under applicable non-bankruptcy law is not enforceable against the estate in bankruptcy (11 U.S.C. §502(b)(1)). In the parlance of the bankruptcy courts, such a claim is not "allowed" (11 U.S.C. §502(a)). To the extent that a debtor could interpose certain defenses against paying a pre-bankruptcy obligation, the estate succeeds to those same defenses and the claim is thereby diminished (11 U.S.C. §502(b)(1)). So, for example, if the pre-bankruptcy business purchases goods that turn out to be defective, the estate's obligation to pay the bill for those goods will be reduced by any unsatisfied breach of contract or warranty claims the business would have had.

Although a claim against the estate is generally allowed in an amount equal to whatever the creditor could have commanded outside bankruptcy, some distributional aspects of the bankruptcy system appear at the claim-valuation stage as well. A few claims are limited in bankruptcy even though they might have been fully collectible otherwise. Claims for the services of an insider or an attorney of the debtor may not exceed "the reasonable value of such services" (11 U.S.C. §502(b)(4)). This permits the court to review the actions of the insiders and attorneys to be certain that they are not draining value from the estate without providing commensurate value. Claims for breach of a lease, for compensation for breach of employment contracts, and for reductions in applicable credits for employment taxes are restricted (11 U.S.C. §502(b)(6), (7), (8)). So, for example, if the business shuts down its operations in a commercial building in breach of a thirty-year lease, the Bankruptcy Code will return possession of the premises to the landlord, but will limit monetary damages to one year's rent payments or 15 percent of the total amount due, not to exceed three years' rent. In these limited circumstances, the court monitors the extent of certain pre-bankruptcy obligations and reduces some of those obligations in the bankruptcy context.

The cleavage that occurs at the filing of bankruptcy is illustrated by yet another aspect of the claims-valuation process. Because claims are valued as of the time of filing, interest provided for by contract but not yet earned will be excluded from a general creditor's allowed claim, whereas interest earned before the filing will be part of that claim (11 U.S.C. §502(b)(2)). This means, for example, that the principal balance on a loan and the unpaid interest that has accrued up to the moment of the bankruptcy filing will be part of the claim, but no interest will continue to accrue after the filing. This provision has an important distributional impact. By mandating that all the unsecured creditors experience the consequences of any delay in the bankruptcy proceedings in the same way, the Code places all of them — tort creditors and contract creditors, creditors with favorable interest terms and creditors with no interest terms — in equivalent circumstances, although they would not all have fared alike outside bankruptcy. If the debtor cannot pay everyone in full, then the unsecured creditors collect no interest after filing, regardless of what their contracts provide. The bankruptcy maxim "equity is equality" is strongest in this forced equality among general creditors once the business has put them all in the bankruptcy boat.

Secured and Unsecured Claims

But just as the theme of "equity is equality" becomes strongest, bankruptcy law reverses course, permitting a huge difference in treatment between two basic classes of creditors: those with properly perfected security interests and those without them. The basis for the difference has its roots in non-bankruptcy law. At state law, secured creditors have greatly enhanced collection rights. There has been a vigorous academic dispute over the rationale for security. Some commentators argue that it promotes more efficient lending markets. Others argue that the low costs of secured lending are offset by the concomitantly higher costs of unsecured lending. Nonetheless, security interests enjoy historical protection, and business practices have embedded such devices in standard commercial transactions. Bankruptcy law extends their protection, so that creditors with security interests generally enjoy better protection in bankruptcy than those without them.

As a bankruptcy case proceeds, the Code distinguishes sharply between secured creditors and unsecured creditors. At the instant of filing, the claims of unsecured creditors are frozen: they can claim the principal amount outstanding plus interest accrued at the time of filing (11 U.S.C. §502). Secured creditors, by contrast, receive an "allowed secured claim," which permits them to claim more than a proportionate share with all the general unsecured creditors. An allowed secured claim is calculated according to the value of the collateral that is covered by the lien or the amount that is subject to a setoff (11 U.S.C. §506(a)). For the creditor whose debt is less than or equal to the value of the collateral, the claim is fully secured. For the creditor whose claim at the time of the filing of the bankruptcy is greater than the value of the collateral, the claim is bifurcated into a secured portion (equal to the value of the collateral) and an unsecured portion (the remaining debt) (11 U.S.C. §506(a)). So, for example, if the business owns a drill press worth $100,000 subject to a security interest and a loan of $80,000, the allowed secured claim is $80,000 in bankruptcy. If, however, the loan is $120,000, the lender's allowed secured claim is limited to $100,000 (the value of the collateral), and the creditor has a general unsecured claim for the remaining $20,000.

In order to confirm a plan of reorganization later on, the secured portion of the claim must be paid in full, while the unsecured portion may be written down. If the estate cannot pay everyone in full — a common outcome in bankruptcy — then the distinction will mean the difference for the creditor between getting paid and taking a substantial loss.

Although the allowed claim of an unsecured creditor is fixed at the bankruptcy filing, the secured creditor's claim may continue to grow. Interest that accrues during the pending bankruptcy will be added to the secured creditor's claim — as will the fees, costs, and charges of collection provided for in the pre-bankruptcy contract — up to the point at which the collateral value is exhausted (11 U.S.C. §506(b)). In terms of distribution, just as secured creditors do better than unsecured creditors, oversecured creditors do better than undersecured creditors.

Estimation of secured claims is necessarily more complex than estimation of unsecured claims. With secured claims, the court must determine not only the amount owed to the creditor, but also the value of the collateral. The Code directs that collateral is to be valued "in light of the purpose of the valuation and of the proposed disposition," suggesting that a liquidation valuation would be appropriate in a liquidation proceeding and that a going-concern valuation would be appropriate in the reorganization context (11 U.S.C. §506(a)). Collateral valuation thus determines whether a claim is fully secured or is bifurcated into secured claims and unsecured claims. A creditor owed a debt of $80,000 secured by a machine valued at $100,000 has a fully secured claim and the opportunity to accrue up to $20,000 of post-petition interest, fees, and costs. If the debt were $120,000, the same creditor would have an allowed secured claim of only $100,000, an unsecured claim of $20,000, and no entitlement to post-filing interest (11 U.S.C. §§506(a), 502(a)).

The court must also decide whether the creditor's claim of security is valid. A detailed discussion of the debtor's abilities to attack outstanding security interests is provided in Chapter 4; however, it is important to note here that these abilities are quite potent: When the debtor is able to avoid a security interest in bankruptcy, the underlying claim against the estate is demoted to unsecured status.

After the secured claims are calculated, it is time to deal with the unsecured claims. Even those claims are not treated precisely the same. Priority unsecured claims are a special class of claims that will be paid in full before any distribution is made to the general unsecured claims. Taxes and unpaid employee wages are the most frequently occurring priority debts. For purposes of understanding the rights of the parties at the inception of the bankruptcy, however, the key distinction is the larger one between secured creditors and unsecured creditors.

POLICY CONSIDERATIONS

At the instant of filing, the relationship between the old debtor and its creditors is transformed. Until the filing, the relationship is governed by a general collection system of "each creditor for itself," and the debtor is able to resist some creditors, pay others, and manage its assets as it sees fit. Then, at the moment of filing, creditors' actions move from individualistic to collective. Instead of making their own decisions about collection calls and repossession, threats and refinancing, creditors are instantly embedded in a collective proceeding. Creditors' rights in bankruptcy are determined by overriding federal law, a law that is written in the explicit context of knowing that assets are too few to pay everyone in full. No creditor can take more than its predetermined share. The automatic stay is critical to the Code's collective proceeding, permitting only limited exceptions for individual creditor action.

The automatic stay serves, metaphorically, to lock all the doors and windows of the newly created bankruptcy estate until the assets can be accounted for and rational decisions about their distribution can be made. Because old management of the business is typically left in place,[12] especially during the period immediately following the bankruptcy filing, this period is often referred to as a "breathing space" for management to hold off collection attempts and to prevent the estate from being dismantled while it plans a strategy to improve the value of the business.

Like the provisions creating the automatic stay, the provisions determining what property will constitute "property of the estate" are written broadly. The policy considerations are similar. The Code, by giving the broadest possible definition to "property of the estate," enables the estate to retain property that may be used to enhance the value of the estate in a subsequent sale or reorganization. Such a move increases the distribution to the creditors, permitting them to capture the going-concern value of the business, rather than the liquidation value of the disparate pieces. Moreover, a broad sweep brings all the property into the estate for distribution according to bankruptcy priorities.

The collective nature of a bankruptcy proceeding is also reflected in the broad definition of property of the estate. The estate is constructed for the benefit of the creditors as a group. Because the estate is granted interests in property superior to those that the pre-bankruptcy debtor could enforce, the estate is better able to safeguard the collective rights of the creditors by denying any single creditor a disproportionate share of the available resources. The estate includes all the business's property, all legal and economic interests of the debtor, and even rights that the creditors would have against other creditors.

The claims process enforces a similar collectivization. Claims against a debtor are transformed into claims against an estate, which gives the court the opportunity to supervise the accounting, monitoring and valuing each charge against the estate's assets. The claims process works in tandem with the automatic stay to encourage a carefully planned administration of the interim bankruptcy estate, aiming the bankruptcy reorganization process toward enhancing the value of the bankrupt debtor and the equitable distribution of its assets.

Eventually the creditor with a valid security interest will retain an *in rem* right against collateral. That means that once the plan is confirmed, unless other provisions have already been made, the creditor will be able to collect the debt by seizing and selling the property under state law. But even if the sale produces a loss, any liability of the pre-bankruptcy debtor will be gone. The claims process takes all of the personal liability of the business and translates it into claims against the estate. In addition, while the case is pending, the automatic stay preserves the property for the use of the business — and the benefit of all the creditors.

The claims process is critical to the distributional objectives of the Code. As claims are estimated, valued, and assigned certain priority rights, the distributional scheme of the bankruptcy system comes to life. Whether an obligation owed by a debtor becomes a claim — and can thus be discharged — raises a critical distributional question among competing creditors. Similarly, the discharge of claims or the rewriting of payment obligations over time necessarily distributes the assets of the estate among competing parties.

The automatic stay, creation of the bankruptcy estate, and transformation of obligations owed by the debtor into claims against the estate are the foundational tools for exercising control over both the assets and activities of the failing business. In order to preserve the value of the business and to give it a chance to reorganize, these powerful tools are handed to the estate in the hope that, by the end of the process, there will be more value for everyone. And, to make certain that no one crowds to the front of the line or slips property out the back door, these tools protect the new distributional scheme imposed by bankruptcy law.

CONCLUSION

A profound shift in the relationship between debtors and creditors occurs at the filing of a bankruptcy petition. A bankruptcy estate is created, comprising both the legal and economic interests of the old debtor and the collective economic and legal interests of the creditors. Creditors lose their individual collection rights against the business. Instead, they must now deal with an estate operating on behalf of all the creditors, trading their pre-petition debts for claims against the bankruptcy estate. A powerful automatic stay stops all efforts to collect individually from the estate and its property. In this way, the bankruptcy system offers an opportunity to enhance value by creating and protecting the new estate. The distributional objectives of the Code also begin to surface at the inception of the case, providing comparatively better rights for the secured creditors but imposing pro rata distribution among the unsecured creditors.

~ 3 ~

Operating the Business

For most businesses, closing down operations even temporarily would be a death knell. Customers go elsewhere. Employees leave. Rumors swirl. Creditors panic. To preserve going-concern value in a business, it is essential that the business remain a going concern. Chapter 11 is built around that critical insight.

When the business files for bankruptcy, it remains open for business. The automatic stay is in place to protect the estate against creditor collection actions, but that does not keep everything humming. The business must still pay the expenses of daily operation and generally prove its value if it is to have a successful reorganization. This chapter offers a brief look at how the business functions in Chapter 11.

WHO RUNS THE SHOW?

There are two likely candidates to run the post-filing Chapter 11 business: the management of the old, pre-filing debtor, or a trustee appointed by the court. The trustee would have full control over the business, like the management team of the pre-bankrupt debtor, and would be obligated to file reports and otherwise move the business toward liquidation or reorganization.

Through the years, the American bankruptcy system has reflected different approaches to the question of who should be left in control of the bankrupt business. Under the 1898 Act, as amended in 1938, a trustee was appointed in large businesses' reorganizations (the old Chapter X), whereas old management remained officially in control only in small businesses' reorganizations (the old Chapter XI). Dissatisfaction with this scheme was widespread. It spurred the development of a complex jurisprudence to classify "large" and "small" businesses, as firms labored mightily to avoid Chapter X and to get into Chapter XI (and thereby retain current management). In addition, many argued that the cumbersome Chapter X process of appointing a receiver and changing the management of a business just as it underwent financial upheaval was wasteful and contributed to the downfall of faltering businesses. These concerns prompted one of the key changes implemented in the 1978 Code: creation of the Debtor-in-Possession (DIP) to run the post-bankruptcy business.

MANAGING AS A DEBTOR-IN-POSSESSION (DIP)

When a business files for bankruptcy, the old management team automatically becomes the management of the new DIP. By operation of law, the DIP serves as the trustee in a Chapter 11 case (11 U.S.C. §1107). With only a few exceptions, the DIP has all the rights of a trustee, but it also has all the burdens (11 U.S.C. §1107(a)). Among the trustee's — and hence, the DIP's — duties are the following:

- The DIP is responsible for taking care of the estate's property (11 U.S.C. §§1106(a)(1), 704(a)(2)).

- The DIP examines the claims submitted by creditors and opposes those that are improper (11 U.S.C. §§1106(a)(1), 704(a)(5)).
- The DIP furnishes information to all parties in interest about the operation of the estate (11 U.S.C. §§1106(a)(1), 704(a)(7)).
- The DIP files tax reports and makes a final accounting of the estate (11 U.S.C. §§1106(a)(1), 704(a)(8), (a)(9)).

The DIP is excused only from the trustee's obligation to investigate the actions of the debtor, a function that can be performed by an examiner, if one is needed (11 U.S.C. §§1107(a), 1106(a)(3)).

The most important power bestowed on the DIP is the authorization to continue the business. The DIP need not ask the court's permission to do this (11 U.S.C. §1108). Instead, after filing, the business can continue to operate as usual. This permits the debtor to maintain operations so that the business need not be shut down at filing even for a moment. This provision eliminates any lost revenue and avoids damaging the business's prospects even further.

REPLACING THE DIP

As an alternative to the DIP, a trustee in bankruptcy (TIB) may be appointed, but only in extraordinary circumstances. A party in interest must move for such an appointment; the court must then find either that cause exists to replace management or that such an appointment would best serve the creditors, stockholders, and other interests of the estate (11 U.S.C. §1104(a)). Structurally, all powers in Chapter 11 are granted to the trustee, but then the Code gives the DIP the rights, powers, and duties of a trustee (11 U.S.C. §1107).

Typically, a court will consider replacing a DIP with a trustee only at the insistence of a group of creditors or the

U.S. Trustee. The reasons justifying removal of a DIP "for cause" are explicitly defined within the Code to include "fraud, dishonesty, incompetence, or gross mismanagement of the affairs of the debtor by current management, either before or after the commencement of the case." If the facts justify it, the court can replace a bad manager who cannot run the business so as to earn the profits that might otherwise be produced. It can also replace a dishonest manager who may be diverting assets of the business. The Code makes it clear, however, that business failure alone is not a sufficient cause to replace current management (11 U.S.C. §1104(a)). Greater mismanagement than that must be shown.

The second major ground for removing a DIP is set forth in far less detail than the first. If the bankruptcy court finds for any reason that the appointment of a trustee would be in the interests of the creditors or the equity holders, or would serve the other interests of the estate, it has virtually unconstrained power to remove the DIP and appoint a trustee (11 U.S.C. §1104(a)). If, for example, workers were so furious with a management team that personal differences made a successful reorganization unlikely, a judge might consider removal of a DIP without any showing of mismanagement. Here again, the Code displays a certain pragmatism about the intended result — survival of the business. The courts are provided with fairly specific guidance to handle routine cases, but they are empowered to act in any way necessary to accomplish the goals of the reorganization.

A court that is reluctant to appoint a trustee may nonetheless order more careful oversight of the DIP through the appointment of an examiner (11 U.S.C. §1104(c)). An examiner can investigate the debtor and the conduct of the debtor's business affairs (11 U.S.C. §1104(c)). In large business reorganizations — those involving unsecured debts greater than $5 million — the Code provides for appointment of an examiner whenever a creditor requests one (11 U.S.C. §1104(c)). In the reorganizations of smaller businesses, an examiner is appointed only when the court determines that it is in the interests of the creditors, equity holders, or other interests of the estate. Thus the big cases, once automatically slated for a trustee, can now be investigated by an examiner whenever a creditor wants one, and the small cases can be investigated when the court finds reason to do so.

Bankruptcy is full of practical realities, however, and those with the money often call the shots. A creditor that plans to offer substantial amounts of post-petition financing for the business can often name the management team. The leverage is clear: If the creditor is not comfortable with the management, then the creditor need not put its money into the business reorganization. Old creditors that do not have any plans to invest in the flailing business are stuck with old management or can try for a trustee, but those with the choice to invest new money or not are in a very different position.

Similarly, anything else that gives a creditor leverage may also affect who sits in the management chair, or, more accurately, the new loyalties of the manager. So, for example, a secured creditor with the power to demand high post-petition payments or a labor union with the ability to call a strike may have important influence over who runs the show and how they run it.

The question of who exercises control in a Chapter 11 case has provoked a spirited debate among prominent academics. Professor Jay Westbrook argues that in recent years large Chapter 11s have succumbed to the control of secured creditors, raising serious questions in his mind about the whether the collective goals of reorganization are met.[1] Professors Douglas Baird and Robert Rasmussen arrive at the same conclusion that creditors are moving into control, but they see this as an occasion for celebration.[2]

THE U.S. TRUSTEE

The 1978 Code imposed specific duties on the DIP, but it also created a new entity to perform a number of tasks, including watching over DIPs generally. The U.S. Trustee (the UST) is a government official appointed by the Attorney General for a five-year term to serve various administrative and monitoring functions in the bankruptcy courts of a particular region (28 U.S.C. §581). The UST's office, like a U.S. Attorney's office, serves as a local branch of the Department of Justice. One difference is that there is not a UST for each federal judicial district; only twenty-one USTs cover the entire country. While some USTs are responsible for only one judicial district, most have jurisdiction over more than one district, and several have more than one state to supervise (28 U.S.C. §581(a)).

The UST's responsibilities are detailed in the statute (28 U.S.C. §586). The UST maintains and supervises a panel of private trustees who will be eligible to serve when appointed by the court. The UST exercises some supervision and monitoring, and can enter a case to participate in any dispute or to raise its own objections if the parties are not following the bankruptcy rules. The UST is responsible for appointing the members of creditors' committees in Chapter 11 and ensuring compliance generally with the rules of bankruptcy (28 U.S.C. §586(a)(3)(A)).

Despite the fact that the "T" stands for "trustee" in both cases, it is important not to confuse the Trustee in Bankruptcy (the TIB), a private citizen who is appointed to serve as trustee in a particular bankruptcy case, with the UST. The UST is a government official with some supervisory role, while the TIB is responsible for the day-to-day operations of cases in which he or she has been appointed. Every Chapter 11 case can expect some monitoring by the UST, although the degree and the focus may vary widely. But only in the rare case in which a DIP is ousted from control is the business run by a TIB.

FIRST DAY ORDERS

Management has the right to keep the business open, but in order to keep it running, some orders from the court may be necessary. These orders, often issued at the inception of the case, are called First Day Orders, a sort of house-keeping sounding event that keeps the business open and leaves the more important business decisions for later. Among the orders that may be signed at the inception of the case are provisions to hire the debtor's attorney as the attorney for the bankrupt estate, orders to pay employees their wages as they come due, and terms under which the debtor can use cash collateral.

The First Day Orders are routinely entered without notice or an opportunity to be heard for many of the stakeholders in a Chapter 11 debtor. It may even be obtained ex parte, but more often it will be presented to the court with the largest creditors and perhaps even a critical customer or two in attendance. If a creditors' committee has already been formed, someone from that group will usually attend as well. Of course, those who are sure to get notice of this initial hearing and even a phone call from the business asking them to attend are likely to be those who support the First Day Orders.

The order is typically temporary, set to expire if it is not renewed. Notwithstanding all the indicia of a transitory event, First Day Orders can have an important effect on shaping the estate. The rights and practices established in the orders are often difficult to alter at a later time. The money is often gone, and it can be difficult to recover. The result is that the debtor and a few other crucial players may have a decisive influence on the future of the case and the company, a control that even the court may find difficult to take back.

Through the years, businesses have increasingly used First Day Orders to prefer some creditors over other or to push a plan along a particular line, long before the other creditors have had a chance to explore alternatives. In Chapter 11, the skirmishes begin early.

WHO RUNS THE BUSINESS?

Disputes among the parties over the operation of the Chapter 11 business can run the gamut from disagreements over minor aspects of daily operations to allegations of dishonesty and unfair dealing. Often a dispute over who runs the business is a dispute over the central question of whether the business should be run at all or whether it should be liquidated instead. At other times, disputes over interim operations are distributional disputes in which the central (but often unspoken) issue is whether the business is being run in a way that may profit some creditors at the expense of others.

To leave the old management in control as DIP is to run a number of risks. Old management, after all, often comprises the same folks who brought the business to the brink of collapse, which may not be a strong endorsement for their management skills and business acumen. More important, old management may have incentives that are at odds with those articulated in the bankruptcy system. There are any number of ways in which the efforts of old management to retain its jobs and its perquisites of office can create costs that are ultimately borne by creditors, shareholders, or both. For example, old management will usually participate in negotiations for a refinancing the business. The lender that plans to provide that refinancing may make it known that favorable terms for the lender will increase the odds that the lender will recommend that the management team stay on post-bankruptcy — an issue over which a new lender may have a surprising amount of influence.

Recent studies show that the CEO of a large business who presides over its demise will often be replaced either just before filing or shortly thereafter. Professors LoPucki and Whitford studied the largest Chapter 11 cases in the 1980s and found a turnover rate of 95 percent for top management during the eighteen months before a bankruptcy filing and the six months following a filing.[3] Professor Betker reported that only 9 percent of the top managers in 202 publicly traded companies still had their jobs two years after a bankruptcy filing.[4] Professor Gilson examined 409 publicly traded companies from the 1980s and reported that 71 percent of managers lost their jobs within two years following a bankruptcy filing, compared with replacement rates of about 3–10 percent in other companies.[5] In small Chapter 11 bankruptcies, however, which constitute the bulk of filings, old management tends to remain entrenched throughout the bankruptcy proceedings.[6] The harsh reality of likely replacement in the big cases and the comforting assurance of staying in charge in small cases lurk in the background of every filing decision undertaken by a soon-to-be DIP.[7]

Angling to be installed as the new management of the estate, old management has an incentive to continue business operations past the point at which the value of the estate begins to dissipate. In some cases, when it becomes clear that the business cannot succeed, quickly liquidating the company might permit a greater payment to the creditors but offers nothing to the departing managers. Moreover, old management's primary loyalty may be to the new investors who fund the reorganization, even if that loyalty is not conducive to increasing the value of the estate for distribution to the old creditors. In the reorganizations of large businesses, old management may contemplate a management buyout or a stock compensation plan, pitting it directly against the old equity holders and possibly the creditors as well. In smaller businesses, where the old equity holder and the manager are often the same person, the entire thrust of the reorganization may be to find a way for the old equity holder to emerge as the owner of the reorganized business regardless of the effect on creditors (or, for that matter, regardless of the effect on the business itself). In a number of cases, involving both large and small businesses, old management has fought single-mindedly to resist any plan that would involve its replacement by a new management team. These conflicts of interest may be kept in the background and settlements may be reached amicably, or they may become hotly disputed and provoke bitter fights.

Even the most scrupulously fair DIP will face the intractable problem that different classes of creditors have conflicting interests, putting management in a virtually impossible situation. The fully secured creditor, for example, may stand to recover completely in an immediate liquidation, while giving the business a chance to reorganize carries the risk that the collateral will decline in value and leave the creditor with only a fraction of its debt paid off. This fully secured creditor often has much to lose and little to gain by supporting the efforts to reorganize. By contrast, the unsecured creditor who would be paid nothing on liquidation has a keen interest in seeing the business continue. The unsecured creditor may have nothing more to lose and will therefore will see substantial benefit if the reorganization is even modestly successful. Other parties — those who buy and sell to the Chapter 11 business, those who are employed by the business, or those who collect taxes from it — may also want to see the business continue. Seeing few pitfalls and plenty of benefits for themselves, they may support efforts to essentially gamble for recovery with the property of the estate. Lacking a single "creditor position" to guide it, the DIP is placed in the position of trying to satisfy a number of conflicting interests that often may be impossible to reconcile.

Standing alone, these factors might support replacing old management in virtually every case, but the new management would face the same conflicts. Besides, replacing management carries costs of its own. To bring in a trustee at the moment of the bankruptcy filing would be to switch management precisely when the business is at its most precarious point.

Confusion over the effects of the bankruptcy filing is at its peak. New payment arrangements with suppliers and employees often need to be negotiated. Decisions that are crucial to the business's survival, such as which business lines to continue and which to abandon, must be made quickly. To make these decisions and to implement them swiftly requires intimate familiarity with all the operations of the business. It can be extraordinarily difficult to find a trustee familiar with the details of a particular business in a short time. In fact, management desertions in Chapter 11 tend to hamper reorganization efforts, not help them. Ousting a management group that is willing to stay on may sometimes eliminate whatever value the going-concern business might have had.

Retention of current management serves other Code goals as well. Although the decision to file for bankruptcy is reserved to the board of directors, managers are typically the ones who frame much of the debate. If managers know it is virtually certain that they will be replaced in Chapter 11 even if they are doing a good job in trying to turn around a troubled business, they will be disinclined to file even if it would be the wisest course for the business. As a result, fewer companies would choose bankruptcy, and more companies would delay filing until the business no longer had any reasonable prospect for reorganization. With fewer and later filings, whatever wealth-enhancing effects the reorganization of troubled businesses in Chapter 11 might offer would be drastically reduced. Moreover, the distributional objectives of the bankruptcy system would be forfeited, leaving the swiftest or strongest creditors to seize all the assets.

Management may understand that a Chapter 11 filing is likely to be bad for their careers, but some chance to save their jobs probably looks much better than no chance at all. Permitting those who make the bankruptcy filing decision to remain in control after filing increases the odds that bankruptcy will be a viable alternative for businesses in trouble.

Sometimes the manager who makes the decision to file for Chapter 11 is not the same manager who rode the business downhill, especially in public companies. Over the past ten years or so, a new professional has emerged to serve the troubled business. Turnaround management firms are consultants who manage businesses in financial distress, often taking them through bankruptcy for a thorough cleaning before the businesses are stabilized and the management team flies off to another crisis. These specialists have become a sufficiently important part of the overall restructuring dynamic that they have even developed their own trade association, Turnaround Management Association (TMA).

In public companies, the development of turnaround management (TM) specialists has further changed the dynamics regarding when and whether to seek either a trustee or an examiner. TM specialists advertise their successes in temporarily taking over failing businesses on short notice in a wide variety of industries, providing stability, vision, and leadership to get the company out of its present hole.

TM is not a business for the faint of heart, and, despite some claims, the practitioners cannot turn dross into gold. TM is also very expensive, making it applicable primarily to businesses of substantial size. But the presence of TM means that courts and creditors have somewhere else to turn when they lose faith in current management. In recent years, turnaround managers have served as trustees, as examiners, and as consensual replacement management in some of the largest business reorganizations.

For smaller companies, where there is less creditor involvement and where there may be no business without the personal involvement of the owner-operator, the presumption of continuing control in Chapter 11 accords with both the policy and the reality of such cases. There is little reason to believe that managers of small companies are routinely replaced. This difference highlights a distinction between small and large Chapter 11s that is largely ignored in the policy debates; we should keep in mind that general statements based on one set of experiences may well be completely inapplicable to Chapter 11s of a different size.

The Code's drafters were convinced that the system would usually operate better if current management was left in place. Legislative history shows that the drafters believed such a policy would generally enhance the value of the estate as well as encourage more troubled businesses to file for Chapter 11. But they also recognized that the consequences of leaving management in charge could be value-reducing and that mechanisms were needed to control and, if necessary, to replace management in such cases. Moreover, they recognized that unintended distributional effects might follow from permitting old management to run the post-filing business. Thus, while the Code leaves old management in control as a general rule, it hems in its operation of the business and provides for oversight by the court and the creditors.

Management is permitted to direct the business operations, but it does so with explicit instructions to assume the role of "Debtor-in-Possession": acting on behalf of all interested parties, not simply itself or the old equity holders it once represented. The DIP, for example, can operate the business *only* in the ordinary course without court approval, and it must negotiate either a consensual plan or a plan that pays all creditors in full before old equity holders retain any ownership. The DIP is in control of the day-to-day operations, but the Code is replete with specific checks to ensure that creditor interests are appropriately protected.

ROLE OF THE CREDITORS

Although old management remains in control and the business continues to operate, post-filing operations take place in a milieu very different from that which preceded the bankruptcy filing. On the one hand, the creditors are prevented from pursuing collection activities, forcing them to take a hands-off approach to the business's property. On the other hand, the creditors collectively are given much greater leeway to examine the business and, in proper circumstances, to demand its outright liquidation.

Committee Work

The U.S. Trustee convenes a meeting of creditors in every Chapter 11 case (11 U.S.C. §341(a)). The trustee may also call a meeting of equity holders, but it rarely does so (11 U.S.C. §341(b)). The single most important committee is the creditors' committee, which is composed of creditors that hold unsecured claims (11 U.S.C. §§1102, 1103). Other committees may be formed for equity holders or even some subset of unsecured creditors (such as tort claimants or pension fund beneficiaries) (11 U.S.C. §1102(a)(2)). Secured creditors have unique interests in their separate collateral, with each secured creditor hostile to all the other secured creditors and to all the unsecured creditors. As a result, secured creditors don't join others on committees. The unsecured creditors' committee, along with any other committees formed, is intended to play a key role in the Chapter 11 process.

The creditors' committee is given the opportunity to monitor the activities of the DIP. To assist it in that role, the committee may seek court approval for the selection of lawyers, accountants, and other professionals to represent its interests (11 U.S.C. §1103(a), (b)). Expenses of the professionals are reviewed by the court and paid out of the estate as an administrative priority expense (11 U.S.C. §§507(a)(2), 1103(a)). Thus, creditors are encouraged to act collectively to reduce expenses and to balance the power held by the DIP.

The creditors' committee is a "party in interest" with the right to be heard on any issue, to request the appointment of a trustee or examiner, and to move to convert the Chapter 11 proceeding to a Chapter 7 liquidation (11 U.S.C. §§1109(b), 1103(c)(4), 1104(a), 1112(b)). The committee can consult with the DIP concerning administration of the case — and the DIP, for its part, is required to meet with the committee (11 U.S.C. §1103(c)(1), (d)). Furthermore, the committee is specifically authorized to inquire into the acts, conduct, assets, liabilities, and financial condition of the debtor, and to investigate the operation of the debtor's business (11 U.S.C. §1103(c)(2)). It is also charged with the responsibility of examining the desirability of continuing the business and any other matter relevant to the formulation of the reorganization plan (11 U.S.C. §1103(c)(2)). Moreover, the committee is permitted to participate in negotiating the plan and to recommend whether the plan should be accepted or rejected by those it represents (11 U.S.C. §1103(c)(3)). Finally, to make certain that it can operate effectively to balance the powers of the DIP, the committee is given the power to "perform such other services as are in the interest of those represented" (11 U.S.C. §1103(c)(5)).

Despite the strong role carved out for the creditors' committee, creditors need not operate solely within this structure to exercise some power over the functioning of the estate. Any single creditor is a "party in interest" in Chapter 11 and, as such, may seek the appointment of a trustee or examiner, move to liquidate the estate in Chapter 7, or object to the plan (11 U.S.C. §§1109(b), 1104, 1112, 1128). Special provision is made for participation by the Securities and Exchange Commission, which can appear and be heard on any issue in Chapter 11 but cannot appeal from the bankruptcy court's judgments (11 U.S.C. §1109(a)). Such participation has declined in recent years, although there has been some recent discussion of the SEC's taking a more active role, particularly in cases involving stock trading.

The Code is clearly set up to strengthen the creditors' role through a creditors' committee and thereby to balance the power given to the DIP. In reality, only the largest cases tend to have active creditors' committees. In such cases, the committee can be tremendously influential. For example, in very large Chapter 11 cases, a creditors' committee wields such power that a debtor rarely proposes a plan for confirmation without having first obtained the committee's endorsement. The situation in small Chapter 11 cases is very different. Most U.S. trustees report that in typical cases no creditor is willing to serve on a committee because the amounts at stake and the assets likely to come from the reorganization are too small to justify the amount of time the creditor would have to spend. In practice, large cases differ from small cases, and the potency of the threat of creditor intervention varies dramatically in the two contexts. In small cases, the DIP typically manages the business with little interference from the unsecured creditors, while the number of backseat drivers goes up as the size of the business increases.

Structurally, the Code balances the disparate interests in a Chapter 11 reorganization effort by creating a dynamic tension. The DIP has the power to run the business, but the creditors can investigate how the business is run, move to replace the DIP, recommend liquidation, and participate in the plan process.

HOW THE BUSINESS OPERATES

For nearly all businesses in Chapter 11, the most pressing need is for operating capital. To keep the business going until long-range plans for enhanced profitability can be developed, the debtor must somehow manage to pay its employees, buy supplies, produce the goods and services that keep revenue coming in, and so on. Because uneasy suppliers that once extended credit now demand cash payments, and lines of credit and other financing arrangements quickly dry up, the need for cash after filing a Chapter 11 petition is often greater than it was beforehand. At the same time that the business has an acute need for cash, there is undeniably some risk in giving the debtor control over an asset that can so quickly disappear.

Again, the Bankruptcy Code threads a metaphoric needle. The DIP or TIB is left in control of the business, but neither will be given the free rein to operate in Chapter 11 that the company would have been operated outside bankruptcy. There are two important restrictions placed on the DIP operating in Chapter 11: The DIP is permitted to use cash generated by the business and to use, sell, or lease any property of the estate — so long as the DIP acts "in the ordinary course" of the business's operations (11 U.S.C. §363 (c)). This means, in effect, that the DIP has authority only to continue the ordinary operations of the old debtor. If it wants to sell off some equipment, cease production of a particular product, take up a new line of business, settle a pending dispute, or engage in any other "out of the ordinary" activities, creditors must be notified and given an opportunity to object, and court approval must be obtained (11 U.S.C. §363(b)). The first restriction is aimed generally at preventing the DIP from squandering the estate's assets. The second is focused more narrowly on the use that the DIP makes of cash.

The issue of access to cash is often a life-or-death question for the struggling Chapter 11 business. On the one hand, if the business cannot use its cash even in the ordinary course of its operations, the estate will soon be starved for operating capital and operations will cease. On the other hand, cash, in comparison with other types of assets, is so valuable and so difficult to trace that special measures are necessary to protect the creditors that have bargained for an interest in cash generated by the estate. The Code draws the line by granting the DIP immediate access to cash on which there is no recognized legal encumbrance, while imposing formidable restrictions on the debtor's use of "cash collateral" (11 U.S.C. §363(c)(2)).

Cash collateral consists of the cash and cash equivalents in which a creditor has a recognized security interest (11 U.S.C. §363(a)). When a secured creditor holds a valid security interest in accounts receivable, for example, all cash that is generated as those receivables are paid off becomes cash collateral. Indeed, any time property of the estate that is the subject of a security interest is liquidated, the resulting proceeds become cash collateral — so long as the original lien continues against them. The Code holds that a DIP cannot use cash collateral, even in the ordinary course of its business, unless the court authorizes such use. Authorization may be granted only if the creditor remains adequately protected, a concept developed in the context of the automatic stay and discussed in the next chapter (11 U.S.C. §§363(d), 362(d)).

This restriction on the use of cash collateral creates a sharp distinction between companies that are selling inventory (which is usually covered by a security interest) and businesses that offer services (which cannot be taken as collateral to secure a loan). Often, businesses do both — sales and service, generating post-petition proceeds that are a mixture of cash collateral and unrestricted cash. This creates an opportunity for negotiation — or a need for dispute resolution, depending on the ability of the parties involved to sort out the distinctions amicably.

To avoid leaving an inventory-driven business completely without cash immediately after filing, the debtor can ask the bankruptcy court to hold a preliminary hearing to authorize the use of cash collateral, pending a final hearing with the creditors present. The balance sought to be maintained is clear: The estate, run for the creditors collectively, operates in the ordinary course, and the secured creditor, with an interest in particular property of the estate, can monitor more closely how that property is used, thereby ensuring that its particular interests are protected.

Even with access to the cash generated by the business, the debtor may well need more money to operate during the reorganization effort. The DIP has a fair amount of discretion to arrange for interim financing for the business, since unsecured debt may be incurred as part of the ordinary course of operations of the business (11 U.S.C. §364(a)). This provision is typically used only for trade credit, often the only unsecured credit that is available to a DIP. If it is unable to find adequate unsecured financing, the DIP can attempt to arrange for secured financing. The DIP can negotiate for credit by offering security interests in unencumbered property of the estate, subordinate liens on encumbered property, priming liens that are equal in priority or take precedence over those of current secured creditors, and priority repayment as an administrative expense to be taken out of the general assets of the estate before payment of the unsecured creditors (11 U.S.C. §364(c)). Secured financing can be arranged only with the approval of the bankruptcy court, however, for obvious reasons. These debts will reshape the business, affecting both the assets the estate will have left to distribute and how the estate will distribute those assets. The DIP cannot take a step so important in the operation of the estate without giving creditors an opportunity to examine and object to the proposed financing. Even if the creditors do not act, the DIP will have to provide them with notice and ask for a hearing for the court to approve its proposed financing.

POLICY CONSIDERATIONS

Bankruptcy law might have replaced the managers instantly, as it once did. Creditors might be given more power to snatch up assets. But if the business is to have a chance to survive, then a much more nuanced balance between debtor and creditor is required. In Chapter 11, managers are left in control, and creditors are stripped of their individual rights to sue or seize property, but those debtor-centric benefits are balanced by the creation of new, collective rights for the creditors and by laws that force the DIP to operate under new constraints.

The balance of power in the Code depends in critical part on the interest and involvement of the creditors. The theory is plain. After all, it is the creditors that stand to lose the most if the DIP mismanages the business and stand to gain if the estate is well managed. In fact, however, many Chapter 11 cases proceed with little creditor interest. The Code does not assume, however, that in such circumstances the creditors' rights will simply be lost. Instead, it provides some minimal procedures to protect even inattentive creditors. These features show up in the Code as restrictions on the power of the DIP to run the business and to impose a plan on the creditors, with the ever-present threat of involvement by the United States Trustee. Thus, the creditors can choose to be active, monitoring the debtor closely, perhaps in this way best protecting the value to be distributed in the estate. But even if they choose not to engage in regular monitoring, the Code invites their involvement at key points in the process.

The opposing interests of the unsecured creditors and the secured creditors are also accommodated by this structure. The standard creditors' committee represents the collective interests of the unsecured creditors. The need for collective action here is particularly acute because the distributional policies of the Code require that a benefit gained by one will be shared by all. Secured creditors, by contrast, are given certain rights they can exercise individually. Secured creditors may act in ways that will profit all creditors, for example, by moving to replace an incompetent manager, but they may also want to exercise rights that are at odds with those of the general creditors, for example, by repossessing a piece of collateral that is essential to the operation of the business.

The Code also balances competing interests by leaving a DIP in control of the case, but maintaining a small, continuing threat of replacement by a TIB. The bankruptcy laws reject any notion of retribution against the old management of a failed business. Punishment is likely to yield little value for the creditors. Instead, the operation of the business turns almost exclusively on the question of what will be best for the going-forward business. In some cases that means a TIB who will bring independence to the role and encourage creditor confidence. In most cases, however, that will mean leaving in place a DIP who knows all the operations in order to carry out a plan to save the business.

Regardless of how the details play out, the structure is designed to permit the efficient operation of the business, clearly in the hope that this will add value.

CONCLUSION

The amount paid to the creditors in Chapter 11 depends in large part on the success of the business's ongoing operations, or, in the alternative, on its efficient, expeditious liquidation. The mechanism the Code relies on to ensure that the best course is followed is, in a sense, enlightened self-interest. The Code purposefully creates a tension by putting power in the hands of both the DIP and all the creditors. It provides rules to control and direct this tension in an attempt to prevent unfair advantage while it permits the managed resolution of conflict in ways that will be of general benefit to the estate.

The issues that emerge in the context of running the business echo throughout the Code, particularly when the rights of individual secured creditors are pitted against the collective interests of the unsecured creditors and the interests of the employees, trade suppliers, customers, and taxing authorities that hope for the successful reorganization of the business. These issues reappear with particular intensity at the plan-confirmation stage, when final agreements among the parties are hammered out.

~ 4 ~

Reshaping the Business

T he automatic stay protects the bankrupt business and provides time to develop a plan of reorganization. The DIP is empowered to continue operating the business, thereby preserving its going-concern value. But for the business to survive and prosper, the DIP often needs to change business operations. The Bankruptcy Code gives the DIP broad powers to redesign the bankrupt estate. These provisions permit the DIP to assume, to assign, and to reject executory contracts; to set aside unrecorded security interests; to recover certain preferential payments and fraudulent conveyances; and to subordinate the debts of certain creditors. These powers reconfigure the relationship between the new bankruptcy estate and those who did business with the company before bankruptcy.

The extent to which any particular DIP will use the provisions discussed in this chapter depends on both the business's current obligations and the shape the DIP hopes the new business will take. For some businesses, the principal difficulty is in the enterprise's financial structure: The business cannot meet loan payments as they come due, and debt restructuring is the thrust of the reorganization. In such cases, the business may plan to continue business operations just as they were before the bankruptcy filing. The outstanding contracts may be amicably assumed by the new estate, and the crucial negotiations will be with key lenders over the long-term financial structure. For other businesses, the reverse is true: The business needs to reshape its business operations, with financing only a secondary concern.

Nearly all operational businesses have various contractual obligations outstanding at the time of the Chapter 11 filing. During the course of the reorganization, the entire business operation is recast by the selective rejection or acceptance of its outstanding agreements. Moreover, a number of the business's continuing, post-filing relationships, for example, with trade creditors or long-term financers, may be powerfully affected by how the DIP uses — or threatens to use — the powers granted to reshape the business and reorder its commercial ties.

DEALING WITH THE OUTSTANDING CONTRACTS

The instant of filing for bankruptcy is a critical moment, as the old business loses all its property and the bankruptcy estate comes into existence to assume control of that property. But for virtually every business filing in Chapter 11, that moment will not coincide neatly with the completion of all outstanding contractual obligations. For most businesses, a number of contractual obligations are outstanding at any point in time, often in varying stages of performance or breach. With the legal termination of the old business, the question of how to deal with outstanding contracts arises. Should the new estate be saddled with them, forced to perform at any cost? Or may it escape all obligations, shrugging off the mistakes of a recent past?

Contracts that are executory — that is, contracts that are not yet fully performed on either side — are about the business's past and its future. Claims against the debtor will be locked into place, and the debtor's liabilities will become clearer. But the plan for fixing the business will also be implemented through the judicious use of the tools for dealing with executory contracts. The powers granted in the Code will let the business decide which stores to keep open and which to close, which vendors to continue to do business with and which to give up, which equipment leases to continue and which to terminate — regardless of any long-term contracts the business had signed years in the past. If the business breaches its contracts, there will be damages to pay, but those damages are part of the pro rata payout in the plan. More immediately, the business can begin to reshape itself so that it can prosper in the future.

Basic Structure

In order that all pre-filing claims against the estate can be dealt with at once, the bankruptcy filing accelerates all the business's outstanding obligations, making them ripe for resolution in the bankruptcy case. "Claim" is broadly defined to include every sort of obligation, liquidated and unliquidated, contingent and noncontingent, matured and unmatured, disputed and undisputed, secured and unsecured, legal and equitable (11 U.S.C. §101(5)). This broad definition encompasses every obligation owed by the business under an outstanding contract that it has not yet performed. Thus, the contractual obligations of the pre-bankruptcy business are reduced to claims against the estate for money damages.

Of course, some of the contractual arrangements may be quite valuable. The opportunity to lease space on favorable terms or to buy supplies at last-month's prices may involve commitments to pay, but on balance these contracts could be profitable for the business. These contractual obligations that could be enforced by contract outside bankruptcy become property of the estate. By this mechanism, valuable contracts enter the estate.

The Bankruptcy Code authorizes the DIP to assume, assign, or reject the old business's contracts as the interests of the estate may require. When the estate "assumes" a contract, it garners the benefits of the contract but it also becomes liable to meet the business's commitments under the contract, including paying the other party to the contract ahead of the general creditors. When the estate assigns the contract, a third party steps in to perform. And when the estate rejects a contract, the estate effectively breaches the contract, leaving the other party to the contract with nothing more than a claim against the estate.

The decisions to perform or breach each of the outstanding contracts will reshape the business as it goes forward. These decisions are not made in the ordinary course of the debtor's business, so the Code requires that the court retain some supervisory authority over the DIP as these decisions are made. Ultimately, the bankruptcy court will determine whether the DIP's motion to assume, assign, or reject each contract will be approved or denied (11 U.S.C. §§365(a), 541(c)). The creditors will receive notice and an opportunity to be heard. If they object to the direction in which the DIP proposes to move the business through the assumption or the rejection of particular contracts, they can ask the court to deny the DIP's request. Typically, however, the only complainant is the non-debtor party to the contract who would prefer some other outcome than what the DIP has chosen. If the technical requirements (detailed below) are met, the courts use a business-judgment test for determining whether the DIP may assume, assign, or reject a contract. Not surprisingly, that flexible standard often ratifies the decisions of the DIP.

For the DIP to assume, assign, or reject a contract, the contract must be "executory" (11 U.S.C. §365). There is no statutory definition of "executory," but the courts generally use a definition advanced forty years ago by Professor Vern Countryman: An executory contract is one in which obligations of the debtor and the non-debtor party are both so far unperformed that the failure of either to perform would constitute a material breach excusing performance of the other party.[1] The definition left open many opportunities for mischief. Professor Jay Westbrook improved on the analysis, concluding that a threshold requirement of executoriness is misplaced; rather, the proper analysis is whether assumption or rejection will produce a benefit to the estate.[2] If the estate can benefit by assuming the contract of the pre-bankrupt business, then bankruptcy law permits it to do so. If, however, the other party has sent goods to the business, there is only a claim by the seller against the estate. Because there is no benefit for the estate, the Code provisions concerning assumption, assignment, and rejection are no longer applicable in that instance.

Rejection

If the DIP rejects a contract, the estate becomes liable for the damages resulting from its breach. This breach is treated as if it had occurred at the instant just before the filing of the petition, in order to equalize the treatment of claims for the breach of the business's pre-petition contracts (11 U.S.C. §502(g)). Regardless of whether they arose before or after the bankruptcy was filed, all claims become claims against the estate.

In general collection law, a number of different contract remedies may be available, depending on the circumstances. Money damages are typical, but in some cases the parties are entitled to equitable remedies, such as specific performance or injunctive relief. Bankruptcy law reduces all contract claims to claims for money damages (11 U.S.C. §365(g), 502(g)). Even equitable remedies must be translated into some monetary equivalent, and the bankruptcy court estimates the size of the claim to be allowed against the estate (11 U.S.C.

§502(c)(2)). The loss of equitable remedies hits some parties particularly hard, such as the party buying a unique good or hoping to enforce a covenant not to compete. But the Code policy is unmistakable. If parties otherwise entitled to equitable remedies could enforce those remedies while those entitled to money damages were limited to a pro rata distribution, there would be no equality of treatment among essentially similar claimants. To ensure that the losses of bankruptcy are distributed on a pro rata basis, the Code generally takes away equitable remedies and reduces all claims to money damages.[3] Apart from this, contract damages are calculated as they would be outside bankruptcy.

Assumption

If the DIP assumes a contract, the estate becomes obligated to perform according to the contract's terms. A subsequent failure to perform during the bankruptcy case is a breach by the estate (11 U.S.C. §365(g)). Repayment is an administrative expense, and damages are payable in full (11 U.S.C. §365(g)(2)). This gives the non-debtor party to a contract the strongest assurance the estate can offer that either the contract will be performed or the party will collect full compensation for the breach.

The non-debtor party is also protected from the consequences of past breach. For the DIP to assume a contract, all earlier defaults must be cured (11 U.S.C. §365(b)(1)(A)). If the non-debtor party has been injured by an earlier default, the estate must either pay the damages or ensure prompt compensation (11 U.S.C. §365(b)(1)(B)).

Finally, if the pre-bankruptcy debtor had breached the contract and the DIP wanted to assume it, then the estate would need to provide adequate assurance of future performance. This assurance can take many forms, from something as amorphous as showing the court a business plan to posting a bond—all depending on the circumstances (11 U.S.C.

§365(b)(1)(C)). The requirement is much like the requirement under the Uniform Commercial Code that permits contract parties in default to reinstate the contract, if they can show assurances of future performance (U.C.C. §2-609(1)).

The estate's assurances are not, of course, perfect guarantees of its future performance — or its ability to perform. Other parties may well be reluctant to go forward with their own part under a contract with the bankrupt business. Nonetheless, as a matter of federal bankruptcy law, they may have no choice in the matter. Once the DIP has properly assumed a contract, another party's failure to perform will constitute a breach, entitling the estate to collect full contract damages and building up assets of the estate (11 U.S.C. §541(a)(7)).

The Code bolsters the DIP's assumption powers by denying effect to certain contractual provisions that purport to restrict them. Financial-condition clauses may provide that the contract automatically terminates when a bankruptcy case commences, when the business becomes insolvent or financially distressed, or when a trustee or receiver is appointed. Those clauses are all nullified in bankruptcy (11 U.S.C. §§365(b)(2), 365(e), (f), 541(c)). To recognize such contractually defined events of "default" would be to run counter to the most fundamental policies of the Code. The Code prohibits parties from opting out of the bankruptcy system by private agreement, instead binding everyone to deal according to the rules imposed in bankruptcy.

Assignment

Once the estate has assumed a contract, it may assign it to a third party, usually in return for money from the assignee (11 U.S.C. §§365(c), (f)). Such assignment protects the estate's ability to realize the full economic value of each contract. The DIP must meet the requirements for assumption before it may assign the contract, and it must also provide the other party to the contract with adequate assurance of future performance by the assignee, whether or not there has been a breach (11 U.S.C. §365(f)(2)(B)).

After an assignment, the estate is not liable for new defaults (11 U.S.C. §365(k)). Even if the business would have remained liable after the assignment in non-bankruptcy law, the estate can shed its liability on a contract when the court approves the assignment.

The DIP enjoys greater rights than the pre-petition business to assign a contract and thereby realize its economic value. The DIP can assume and assign a contract even if the business expressly consented to a prohibition on assignment in the contract (11 U.S.C. §365(f)(1), (3)). The same is true with respect to applicable non-bankruptcy laws that impose prohibitions on assignments (11 U.S.C. §365(f)(3)). The courts, however, have generally declined to enforce these Code provisions precisely as written. Thus, certain well-established common-law prohibitions on assignment, such as the restrictions on assignment of personal-services contracts, and some important general statutory prohibitions, such as the federal restrictions on assignment of defense contracts, are given effect in bankruptcy notwithstanding the seemingly absolute language of Section 365(f).

Expanding the availability of assignment powers maximizes the value of the estate. Such value obviously may come at the cost of changing the promises outlined in the negotiated contract, but the injury to the non-debtor party is lessened by the retention of the common-law assignment rules. In effect, when common law treats assignment as frustrating the reasonable expectations of the parties, assignments are prohibited; when common law treats the contractual obligations as more nearly fungible, assignment is permitted. Similarly, the statutory restrictions on assignment are honored when they seem to be designed to protect legitimate interests of contracting parties. Not surprisingly, these rules leave the bankruptcy courts with much room for interpretation.

Interim Treatment of Executory Contracts

The DIP is not required to appear before the court immediately after filing to reveal which contracts it proposes to assume, which to assign, and which to reject. To impose such a requirement would impinge on the breathing space provided by the automatic stay and deprive the DIP of the opportunity to make decisions that maximize the value of the estate. Sometimes, however, parties that have dealings pending with the business can be injured during this interim period if they cannot determine the status of their contracts.

The Code expressly limits the time the DIP has to make a decision about a contract in a Chapter 11 proceeding in only one instance. With respect to all non-residential leases, the DIP must assume the contract within 120 days of filing or the contract will be deemed rejected (11 U.S.C. §365(d)(1), (4)). The court may extend that time for cause, but the extension is limited to ninety additional days, unless all parties consent. This position was heavily lobbied for by landlords who want businesses to decide quickly whether to stay or go, but many business lawyers argued that businesses with operations scattered around the country, such as the retailer K-Mart, could not be successfully reorganized if the planners could not have enough time to see if their new ideas for leaving stores open in certain regions or trying new distribution chains would succeed.

For all other contracts, the time limits in Chapter 11 are more fluid. The DIP is required only to assume or to reject all executory contracts before confirmation of the plan, a time that could lie months or even years in the future (11 U.S.C. §365(d)(2)). With no time constraints on the decisions about whether to assume all but the lease contracts, the DIP enjoys maximum flexibility. Of course, that flexibility is purchased at the expense of parties that are left in limbo for a very long time. The non-debtor party to the contract may ask the court to set a time for acceptance or rejection of the contract, but the Code articulates no grounds on which the court should grant or deny such a motion. Generally, the court will give the DIP a reasonable time to decide, taking into consideration the cost imposed on the non-debtor party by delay. The amount of time that is "reasonable" varies greatly from case to case and even from contract to contract within a case.

During the period before the DIP decides to assume or reject an executory contract, he nonetheless is obligated to meet outstanding lease obligations, both for rent on non-residential property and rent on equipment or other goods. On all other obligations, such as the pending purchase or sale of goods, the performance of services and every other kind of contract, the Code is silent about the rights and obligations of the parties to an executory contract during the interim period before acceptance or rejection. Until a contract has been rejected, most courts take the position that the non-debtor party must continue to perform, although there is no direct statutory authority for this position. If the non-debtor party fails to perform, it may be liable for damages incurred even before the DIP accepted the contract. Moreover, the court may order performance under its general equitable powers (11 U.S.C. §105(a)).

Even if the estate has defaulted, the other party to the contract cannot take it for granted that the contract has been rejected. The other party must remember that the DIP has the power to reject a contract only with court approval (11 U.S.C. §365(a)). Moreover, the Code permits the DIP to cure even post-petition defaults in order to assume contracts. The other party thus faces powerful incentives to continue its performance under the contract while it awaits definitive action from the DIP and the bankruptcy court, even if the contract may ultimately be rejected. One source of solace for such a party is that the estate will be liable for the cost of any benefits conferred on it after the bankruptcy filing, and such expenses are payable in full, ahead of the general unsecured creditors (11 U.S.C. §503(b)).

Special Circumstances

The executory contract provisions have become the target of substantial special interest lobbying. Few policymakers would agree to change the general rules of assumption, assignment, and rejection, but Congress has been quite responsive to the demands of special interests. Among the groups enjoying exceptions to the general rules on executory contracts are labor unions, retirees, real estate and time-share landlords, shopping centers, licensees of intellectual properties, and buyers of real estate.

Perhaps the best protection is reserved for lenders with open lines of credit in favor of the pre-bankruptcy business. The Code declares that these contracts for "financial accommodations" cannot be assumed by the DIP (11 U.S.C. §365(c)(2)). Bankruptcy terminates such obligations as a matter of law, whether or not the contract creating them so provides. The business fortunate enough to have a commitment for future financing will forfeit that arrangement when it files for bankruptcy.

The economic policy at work here is hazy at best. A seller of goods is required to deliver on credit when the debtor assumes a contract, even at the risk of losing the value of those goods if the debtor ultimately proves unable to repay. If a lender were forced to lend cash according to its earlier promise, it would run a similar risk. But the Code provisions sharply distinguish between the two, holding the seller to the contract if the debtor assumes it while excusing the lender from any future contract performance. The consequences of this distinction become more conspicuous as debtors come forward with pre-packaged bankruptcy plans under which lenders commit to financing in contemplation of a bankruptcy filing — only to have the Code grant them a right to back out after the business files.

It may be that the drafters of the Code were convinced that financial accommodations contracts should be called off so that the business's post-petition financing arrangements could be scrutinized as a whole. Or it may be that the distinction reflects the idea, pervasive both in commercial law generally and in the Bankruptcy Code specifically, that money is sufficiently volatile and difficult to trace that it should receive special treatment. Or it may reflect the influence of banks and other commercial lenders on congressional legislation. In any case, the provision is difficult to fit into a neat theoretical structure.

Labor union contracts also receive special treatment once the employer files for bankruptcy. Under the 1984 amendments to the Code, the DIP has post-filing obligations to negotiate with the union and to reveal important information about the business (11 U.S.C. §1113(b)). Moreover, the DIP cannot reject a collective bargaining agreement on the simple business judgment test employed generally when the court reviews the business's choices on assumption, assignment, and rejection of ordinary executory contracts (11 U.S.C. §1113). To give extra protection to unionized workers, the Code provides that the DIP may reject a collective bargaining agreement only if "the balance of the equities clearly favors rejection of such agreement" (11 U.S.C. §1113(c)). The distributional intent of this provision is obvious: If possible, unionized employees should suffer less from the business's failure than other creditors should, but they should bear their share of the losses if it is essential for a reorganization of the company.

A similar attempt to offer some protection to a specific group of creditors is evident in restrictions on the rejection of agreements covering retired employees' health and pension benefits. The Code now provides for representation of retirees and for negotiation with the DIP regarding the appropriate level of benefits (11 U.S.C. §1114(b), (c), (d), (f)). The estate is obligated to continue such benefits during the negotiation period, unless the court orders otherwise (11 U.S.C. §1114(e)). Modification of retiree benefits shall be authorized only if the court finds that the proposal is fair and equitable to all the affected parties, is necessary for an effective reorganization, and is "clearly favored by the balance of the equities" (11 U.S.C. §1114(g)). Once again, the distributional intent is clear, this time favoring retired employees who have intact health and pension benefit plans at the time the business files for bankruptcy.

When the bankrupt business is a tenant, the Code is more explicit about the limitations on the scope of the DIP's authority under the executory contract provisions. If a nonresidential lease has terminated pre-petition, a business that rents the property may not cure and assume the contract (11 U.S.C. §365(c) (3)). Moreover, the DIP may not require the landlord to furnish services under an unexpired lease without pre-paying for the services (11 U.S.C. §365(b)(4)). The protection given landlords when their tenants file for bankruptcy is offset by another Code provision. If the tenant files for bankruptcy and rejects its lease, the landlord may file a claim against the estate limited to one year's rent or 15 percent of the remaining lease term, plus any past-due rent (11 U.S.C. §502(b)(6)). The Code also restricts the ability of the landlord to insist on a larger deposit based solely on the DIP's assumption and assignment of the contract (11 U.S.C. §365(l)). The landlord is stuck with whatever would be the ordinary deposit for a similar tenant. This provision prevents the landlord from indirectly avoiding the impact of the assumption and assignment powers given the DIP.

The Bankruptcy Code offers general protection for debtor-lessees, but it imposes specific restrictions on debtors who lease shopping center space. For shopping center leases, adequate assurance of future performance includes consideration of percentage rents, tenant mix, location relative to other businesses, and exclusivity provisions (11 U.S.C. §365(b)(3)). In other words, a bankrupt children's shoe store may have great difficulty getting approval to install a tattoo parlor in its place in the shopping mall if the mall's management objects. This limitation gives the landlord greater discretion in refusing a DIP's proposed assumption and assignment of a shopping center lease.

Debtor-landlords also face some specialized restrictions. The debtor that is a landlord or lessor in a time-share agreement may reject unfavorable leases, but the impact of rejection is somewhat limited. The non-bankrupt tenant may accept the rejection, leave the property, and submit a claim for damages against the estate for breach of the lease, as can any other non-debtor party to a contract that has been rejected in bankruptcy (11 U.S.C. §365(h)(1)(A)(i)).

But the tenant has another option. Despite the wishes of the bankrupt landlord, the tenant may stay and offset the damages it has incurred against the rental obligation it owes to the bankrupt landlord (11 U.S.C. §365(h)(1)(A)(ii), 365(h)(1)(B)). In the latter situation, the lessee must waive any other claim against the estate (11 U.S.C. §365(h)(1)(B)). This additional protection — permitting lessees to finish out their lease terms — gives them some leverage against businesses that might use bankruptcy as a means of clearing out a building quickly.

Similarly, if a seller of real property declares bankruptcy, the buyer who is in possession of the property enjoys greater protection than do most non-debtor parties to an executory contract. If the seller rejects the contract, the buyer may either accept the rejection and file a claim, or the buyer may remain in possession and offset its damages against the payment obligations as they come due (11 U.S.C. §365(i)). If the buyer pays for the property in full, it is entitled to a clear title, in effect nullifying the rejection (11 U.S.C. §365(i)). Once a buyer is in possession of property under a purchase agreement, bankruptcy is not an effective means to recover the property for the estate.

When the debtor is a licensor of intellectual property, the licensee has rights to the license that are similar to those of a buyer of real property or a tenant of property or a time-share interest whenever the debtor rejects the real estate contract or lease. In such a case, the licensee may accept the rejection and file a claim, or it may retain a right to exclusive use of the license, waiving any additional rights to claim or offset damages against the estate and effectively nullifying the debtor's rejection (11 U.S.C. §365(n)).

These provisions on shopping centers, time-shares, real property, and intellectual property were added to the Code in response to industry complaints about bankruptcy "abuses" by bankrupt companies. The characterization of the abuses vary from constituency to constituency, as do the policy rationales for better protection of select groups doing business with parties that declare bankruptcy. All the provisions have clear distributive consequences, favoring one class of creditors over the collective group of creditors. Some of the provisions may have been adopted in response to egregious cases that were not properly decided under the general provisions of executory contract law, whereas others may have been adopted to provide greater assurance to some constituencies and to avert concerns about how courts might deal with these pending cases. In any case, over time the Bankruptcy Code's general rules of operations and distribution have developed more and more exceptions.

The Economics of Contracts with Bankrupt Businesses

Any business can breach its contracts. As Justice Oliver Wendell Holmes pointed out, a contract is only an agreement in the alternative: Do the thing promised or pay the damages caused by the breach.[4] If a business not in bankruptcy breaches its contract and the non-debtor party pursues its rights, the breaching party will pay a legally imposed remedy. The same is true in bankruptcy. The DIP can perform or breach the pre-bankruptcy business's contractual obligations. If it breaches them, the non-debtor party will have a claim against the estate for the contract damages. Unless the parties had made arrangements to secure performance with a right to offset or a security interest, the claim will be an ordinary unsecured claim. The rub, of course, is that outside bankruptcy, the breaching party pays the damages in full, whereas in bankruptcy the business will most likely pay all its creditors only a pro rata distributions of what is owed. The DIP pays for its breach, but it pays in tiny little bankruptcy dollars.

The Code makes it clear that the DIP has the same options to breach the outstanding contractual obligations that a non-bankrupt party would have. A consequence is to reduce those contractual obligations to their bare essentials: unsecured claims against an insolvent estate. That is, of course, all they were before filing as well. To burden the estate with paying all obligations not in breach at the time of filing would promote those claims to priority repayment status, to be paid ahead of other unsecured claims. The Code avoids inequality of distribution among creditors by permitting the estate to abrogate obligations after filing just as the business could abrogate them before filing, so that all unsecured claimants brandishing broken contracts are treated the same by the estate regardless of when the breaches occurred.

A second consequence of permitting post-petition breaches of pre-petition obligations is that the DIP can make rational business decisions about which opportunities to pursue after filing. The DIP has the opportunity to breach contracts that are no longer useful to the estate, permitting a reorganization along new business lines that implement new management decisions. The executory contract provisions are designed to give the DIP the ability to redesign the faltering business.

The DIP can also assume outstanding contracts. Not everyone who has signed a contract with the now-bankrupt business will be delighted by such an assumption. Sometimes the non-debtor party worries about the financial stability of the post-filing debtor. At other times the non-debtor party would like to use the fact of bankruptcy as an excuse to escape from a contract that is profitable to the estate but has become burdensome to the non-debtor party. For example, the non-debtor party may have agreed to sell commodities to the debtor at a price that now appears too low or to buy commodities at a price that now seems too high, and escape from such a contract is usually high on its agenda.

To permit the business to assume a contract profitable to the estate harks back to the concepts that govern the formation of the estate and the determination of what property goes into it. At filing, all legal and equitable interests of the pre-bankrupt business debtor become property of the estate. Because the estate is permitted to assume the outstanding executory contracts, the estate captures the economic value of the contracts for the benefit of all the creditors — rather than the one creditor who happens to be a party to the contract.

If the estate assumes a contract, whatever value it has is accompanied by the burdens of performance. Once the DIP assumes the contract, the estate must abide by the old debtor's contractual agreements, including performance in full and payment in full of any monetary obligations. To enforce the written contract is to capture value already exchanged in the contract; to demand the benefits without assuming the burdens would be to insist on a new agreement that the parties had not negotiated. In part, this represents an application of the standard contract law doctrine that contracts are not severable unless the parties specifically so agree. To enforce an agreement, the enforcer must meet its own obligations.

The circumstances of bankruptcy raise an interesting distinction between contracts that have reciprocal obligations due and contracts in which one party has performed and now awaits performance by the other. The distinction goes to the heart of the debtor-creditor relationship: If the non-debtor party has already extended value (e.g., shipped the goods or lent the money) and is waiting only for payment from the debtor, then the non-debtor party is simply a creditor with a claim. But if the non-debtor party has agreed to extend value only after further performance from the now-bankrupt business, the reciprocal nature of the obligations changes the relationship. Both parties are now creditors and both are debtors with respect to the underlying obligations. In bankruptcy, the estate that wants to capture the value of the non-debtor party's promises needs to meet its own obligations to the non-debtor as well.

The requirement that the estate must assume the obligations of any contract it wants to enforce underscores the fact that the estate is a new entity, able to incur debts and obligated to pay them in its own name. The estate, like any other actor in the business world, makes contracts — or assumes the contracts of its predecessor — in full. And it pays for those obligations in full as administrative expense priority claims.

The complaint is sometimes heard that the bankruptcy scheme permits the DIP to come out ahead no matter what: Contracts that are profitable to the estate are assumed while contracts injurious to the estate are breached. This is a sort of "heads-I-win, tails-you-lose" situation that seems quite unfair to the non-debtor. The difficulty with this analysis is that it misses a central point of all contract law. As Holmes notes, any party at any time may elect to perform its profitable contracts and breach its unprofitable ones, so long as it is willing to face the risk that the contract damages it will have to pay will wipe out the gains it realizes by its breach. In bankruptcy precisely the same option is presented. The difference, of course, is that a damage action against a bankrupt estate is not worth as much as a damage action against a solvent estate. This, however, is a problem facing every claimant against a bankrupt estate: A breach of contract claim is simply not worth as much when the breaching party cannot pay. It is economic reality, not bankruptcy policy, that causes the loss to fall on the non-debtor party to a contract with an insolvent debtor.

A second cause for grumbling is the DIP's ability to assume the agreements of the old business while escaping enforcement of some of the duly negotiated terms of those agreements. There is, of course, no justification for forcing the non-debtor party to perform a contract on terms substantially different from those it had bargained for. But the terms of any individual bargain may affect collection priorities in ways that violate bankruptcy norms. For example, the parties might have agreed to a contract under which the debtor is to buy oranges at $1 per bushel, with a provision that calls off the deal if either party files for bankruptcy. If the market price of oranges had risen to $1.25 by the time of bankruptcy, the DIP would want to assume the contract. But if the termination clause were enforceable, the non-debtor party to the contract would be enabled to escape the consequences of its bad bargain by the fortuity of a bankruptcy filing. The estate would be diminished by losing the valuable contract that would have been enforceable outside bankruptcy, all because it had fallen on hard times in its other affairs — not because of any substantive breach of the oranges contract.

Allowing the non-debtor to escape such a contract clearly violates the value-enhancing norms of bankruptcy. Moreover, if one creditor caught in mid-performance can escape bankruptcy treatment because it had the leverage to insist on a contract provision while no other creditors can opt out of the bankruptcy system, the goal of equality of treatment would be upset. Once again, bankruptcy protects the interests of the creditors collectively by neutralizing the effects of advantages that happen to be enjoyed by an individual creditor. Not surprisingly, "ipso facto" clauses and other similar provisions that permit one party to opt out of the bankruptcy system when a business files are not enforceable under the Code (11 U.S.C. §365(e)(1)).

In some cases, the estate is not able to perform on a valuable contract. In those cases, the only way for the troubled business to realize the full value of the contract is to assign it to another company that can perform, often for a payment to the estate. Contract assignment raises the same questions as contract assumption, especially the question of whether the debtor that assigns its rights is forcing the non-debtor party to perform on a contract that is substantially different from the contract to which it agreed, or whether the non-debtor party who resists assignment is merely an opportunist seeking to avoid the collective action of bankruptcy.

SELLING ASSETS

As part of its efforts to reshape its ongoing business, the debtor can sell off non-productive or over-priced assets. If the business owns property free and clear, it can sell that property outright. So, for example, a business with unproductive land or a business that is closing down one line of operations and has no more need for expensive equipment can sell that property (11 U.S.C. §363(b)). Because such sales are not in the ordinary course of business, it is necessary to gain court approval. At some point, the sales may be significant enough that the creditors will object that the business is carrying out its Chapter 11 plan without having ever put the plan to a vote. The court will decide when the business goes too far. It is critical to see, however, that some reshaping of the business will occur long before any reorganization plan is proposed.

While most sales of assets are simple affairs, conducted with court approval under Section 363(b)(1), the ability to sell property in Chapter 11 sometimes confers a very special benefit. Bankruptcy permits the business to offer a buyer a clean title, free and clear of all liens, approved by a federal judge (11 U.S.C. §363(f)). In a case in which there have been multiple disputes over a piece of property, this assurance adds significantly to the price the item will fetch in a bankruptcy sale.

THE STRONG-ARM CLAUSE

During the course of its operations, a business may enter into a number of agreements that promise certain collection rights to its creditors, such as granting a security interest under Article 9 of the Uniform Commercial Code or giving a real estate mortgage. A security interest or a mortgage gives the favored creditor the right to seize the collateral if the business fails to pay as promised. Under state law, those agreements are good against the business as negotiated. If another creditor crowds in and tries to take the same collateral, the agreements are generally not effective against those competing creditors unless additional steps are taken, such as properly perfecting the security interest or recording the real estate mortgage. Only if the property is locked up with both an agreement (security interest or mortgage) and perfection (usually by filing) will the favored creditor be able to fend off all other creditors.

Once the business files for bankruptcy, the creditors want these negotiated agreements enforced to give them better collection rights against the DIP. The Code provisions that permit the DIP to invalidate certain of these pre-bankruptcy agreements are collectively known as "the strong-arm clause."

Operation of the Strong-Arm Clause

When the estate is created at the instant of filing, the DIP is granted the exclusive right to represent the interests of the creditors collectively. Under the strong-arm clause, the DIP is a hypothetical judgment lien creditor, a hypothetical execution creditor, and a hypothetical bona fide purchaser of real property, able to set aside any transfer of property that these creditors or purchasers could set aside (11 U.S.C. §544(a)). The sweep of these provisions is broad, so that the DIP may avoid any transfer of property of the debtor or any obligation incurred by the debtor if one of the imputed creditors could have avoided it (11 U.S.C. §544(a)).

The status of the hypothetical judgment lien creditor permits the DIP to exercise the rights of the judgment lien creditor at state law at the instant of the bankruptcy filing. An unperfected security interest, for example, is effective against the business but ineffective against a judgment lien creditor under state U.C.C. law (U.C.C. §9-317(a)). In such a case, the DIP preserves the superior interest of the hypothetical judgment lien creditor for the benefit of the estate, and hence for the creditors collectively (11 U.S.C. §550(a)). If state law gives the execution creditor rights superior to those of other creditors, those rights are preserved for the benefit of the estate as well (11 U.S.C. §544(a)(2)). This means, for example, that if a secured creditor had an interest in a piece of machinery, but the interest was unrecorded and therefore vulnerable to attack by a judgment lien creditor under U.C.C. §9-317(a), the DIP could assume the interest of the hypothetical judgment lien creditor in the property and preserve that interest for the estate. In effect, the estate would take the value from the equipment, rather than permitting that value to be seized by the creditor who held an unrecorded security interest.

Land transactions can also be set aside if they would be vulnerable to an attack either by a judgment lien creditor or by a bona fide purchaser for value (11 U.S.C. §544(a)(1), (3)). The extension of the DIP's status to that of a bona fide purchaser extends protection for the bankruptcy estate even in states that do not give judgment lien creditors priority over unrecorded real estate interests. As a practical matter, creditors claiming interests that are good against the debtor business but that are ineffective against other creditors because of defects in perfection will lose those interests. Such creditors then join the ranks of the unsecured creditors.

The strong-arm clause permits the DIP to work within the state law system to create and preserve rights for the estate. Because the state law system is used to develop these rights, the variations in the system that permit unrecorded or late-recorded interests to prevail are controlling in bankruptcy as well. This means, for example, that a buyer in possession of real estate who has no recorded interest but whose open and notorious possession of the property would permit it to prevail over a bona fide purchaser of the real estate at state law would obtain the same result in bankruptcy. While the strong-arm clause gives the DIP the powers certain creditors would have enjoyed at state law, it does not contract or expand the substantive law that determines those rights.

The collective nature of the bankruptcy proceeding changes the DIP's powers in another way. Because the Bankruptcy Code imbues the DIP with the powers of a hypothetical lien creditor, the DIP need not prove that any such creditor actually exists who would be able to attack a security interest, mortgage, or transfer. This means that whenever a transaction is legally vulnerable to a lien creditor, the DIP can set it aside in its entirety.

Because a DIP must stand in the shoes of an actual creditor to invoke Section 544(b) to set aside a transaction, it would be reasonable to suppose that the DIP could avoid a transfer or obligation only to the extent of that actual creditor's claim. The Supreme Court in *Moore v. Bay* held to the contrary: The DIP could avoid the transaction completely, even though the resulting liability might be much larger than the claim of the creditor in whose stead the DIP sued. Furthermore, the transaction was avoided for the benefit of all unsecured creditors, not just that class of creditors who could have brought the avoidance action under state law.

The strong-arm clause demonstrates an important collection feature of the bankruptcy system. A bankruptcy petition, including a petition voluntarily filed by the business, has the same legal effect as if a hypothetical creditor had filed a collection action against the business and instantly taken all steps necessary to perfect its interests against all of the business's property. Because this is an idealized, hypothetical creditor, the DIP can ignore deals negotiated between the business and an individual creditor if those deals were not properly perfected — just as a lien creditor would have been able to do.

The distributional aspects of the strong-arm provisions are obvious. The collective rights of the creditors are preserved in bankruptcy, whereas the individual rights of particular creditors against that collective interest are sharply curtailed. Equality of distribution once again dominates the bankruptcy system.

VOIDABLE PREFERENCES

During the period immediately preceding the bankruptcy filing, creditors often intensify their collection efforts. When they learn that the business is in financial trouble, they may exercise both their extra-legal leverage and their formal collection rights to extract payment or a security interest from the failing company. They do so, in part, in recognition that there is unlikely to be enough money to go around, so they want to beat other creditors who may be closing in on the business's assets. Once the bankruptcy occurs, some creditor collection actions that occurred before filing are honored, while others are set aside. The Code provisions on voidable preferences determine which of those last-minute actions will be allowed to stand after the bankruptcy filing and which will not.

Basic Structure

The DIP can set aside a transfer that occurred before bankruptcy if it is a voidable preference. The qualifications of a voidable preference are set by statute. They are detailed and specific. A voidable preference is:

- a transfer
- of an interest in the debtor's property
- on account of an antecedent debt
- made within the preference period (usually ninety days before bankruptcy)
- while the debtor was insolvent
- to or for the benefit of a creditor
- that permits the creditor to recover more than it would have recovered in liquidation if the transfer had not been made (11 U.S.C. §547(b)).

If any of these elements are absent, the transaction is not a voidable preference. The Code also provides specific exceptions, so that some voidable preferences cannot be set aside (11 U.S.C. §547(c)). It may help to look at each of the seven elements of the rule:

1. The avoided transaction must be a transfer. The Code defines transfer broadly (11 U.S.C. §101(54)). It includes the obvious, such as making a payment on an outstanding loan. Transfers may be voluntary or involuntary, so that statutory liens and judicial liens are both designated as transfers. Receiving any interest in property qualifies as a transfer, which means that taking a security interest or recording that interest to perfect it against other creditors qualifies as a transfer.

The transfer provision is broad enough to encompass not only making payments to creditors and perfecting security interests, but also other activities, such as the business's acquisition of property that becomes subject to a creditor's after-acquired property clause. So, for example, if a business buys more inventory and that inventory is immediately subject to a lender's security interest covering after-acquired property, the purchase of the inventory is a transfer for the benefit of the lender. The transfers can be even more attenuated. A transfer may occur, for example, when the business hires workers to assemble bicycle parts that are subject to a security interest or when the business buys fertilizer and water to grow crops subject to a security interest. Whenever the debtor or creditor engages in some transaction that enhances value for a particular creditor, a transfer has taken place. The only creditor to enjoy some increase in value without a transfer is the creditor who has a security interest in property that simply appreciates by the good fortune of market forces.

2. The transfer must be a transfer of an interest in property of the debtor (11 U.S.C. §547(b)). When the business pays a bill, clearly it transfers an interest in its property. But just as surely, if the creditor records a security interest, the creditor perfects an interest in the property that had belonged to the debtor. If, however, a third party paid the business's obligations, the creditor who was paid off may have done better financially than the other creditors, but it did not benefit from an interest of the debtor. By contrast, if the third party paid off an unsecured debt and received a security interest from the business in return for the payment, the transfer involved an interest of the debtor. Similarly, if the third party simply made a loan to the debtor and the debtor used the funds to pay one creditor rather than another, it is clear that the estate was enhanced (when it received the money) and diminished (when the money went to one creditor rather than another). The business's balance sheet may have remained the same, but the money lent to the business became the property of the business, available for distribution to all the creditors. If the debtor

used that money to pay one creditor, even if that was its announced plan, a transfer of the business's property occurred. Whether the funds from the third party were sufficiently "earmarked" by the parties so that the transaction did not involve a transfer to the estate and a resulting voidable preference has been the subject of hot factual dispute in a number of cases.

3. The transfer must be on account of an antecedent debt (11 U.S.C. §547(b)). A purely cash transaction does not qualify as a transfer. If, for example, a business purchases supplies for cash, the transaction falls outside the reach of the voidable preference provisions. This detail permits the failing business to continue to operate at least on a cash basis. It limits the sweep of voidable preference law to minimize the disruption of commercial life that would be involved in setting aside cash deals. Moreover, the provision permits other simultaneous exchanges, such as granting and recording a security interest in return for new credit. The focus on antecedent debt also emphasizes that these provisions are designed to equalize the treatment of creditors. Other provisions police other kinds of transactions, such as executory contracts and fraudulent conveyances, which do not involve antecedent debt. Together they provide a comprehensive review of the business's prebankruptcy transactions.

4. The "reach-back" period to avoid transfers is limited (11 U.S.C. §547(b)(4)). For most creditors, that period is ninety days—an arbitrary date for fixing which creditors must be treated equally (11 U.S.C. §547(b)(4)(A)). For one class of creditors, however, there is a longer reach-back. Transfers to insiders can be set aside as far back as one year (11 U.S.C. §547(b)(4)(B)). Once again, the Code uses a broad definition to maximize the sweep of the provision. An insider includes (but is not limited to) an affiliate or a director, officer, person in control, general partner, or a relative of any of these people (11 U.S.C. §§101(2), (31)). The longer reach-back for insiders reflects the longer period that insiders can divert assets to themselves without attracting notice from their

creditors. The provision also reflects the concern that insiders, who likely have much better financial information than the creditors, may have moved earlier to benefit themselves at the expense of the business. The provision also reasserts the importance of the Code's distributional objectives by opening to scrutiny the transactions of insiders and the debtor business for a full year before the filing, making them vulnerable to a pro rata distribution.

5. The transfer must be made while the debtor is insolvent (11 U.S.C. §547(b)(3)). This requirement highlights the pre-bankruptcy monitoring aspect of the voidable preference provisions. Payments made while the business is solvent are all right, even if they permit some creditors to do better, whereas payments made once the business is insolvent will subject those recipients to give-backs in bankruptcy. Transactions with faltering businesses, not with businesses that are financially solvent, are scrutinized.

   The test for insolvency for these purposes is whether the business's debts exceed its assets, with assets valued at "fair valuation" (11 U.S.C. §101(32)). The Code presumes that the business was insolvent during the last ninety days before filing, but the presumption can be rebutted (11 U.S.C. §547(f)). For the one-year reach-back against insiders, the presumption of insolvency only runs for the ninety days immediately preceding filing. For transactions involving insiders that occurred between 91 and 365 days before the bankruptcy filing, the DIP will be required to prove insolvency.

6. The transfer must be to or for the benefit of a creditor (11 U.S.C. §547(b)(1)). A creditor is broadly defined as anyone holding a pre-petition claim against the business (11 U.S.C. §101(10)). The creditor need not receive the transfer directly. If the transfer benefited the creditor indirectly, the statutory requirement has been met. As the earlier examples show, the business may acquire property that is subject to the creditor's security interest or spend money to enhance collateral in which the creditor has an interest. Both will be transfers for the benefit of a creditor.

The broad language of "to or for the benefit" of a creditor is clearly designed to extend the sweep of voidable preference law to pick up any transaction that benefits a creditor — whether the transfer was made directly to the creditor or not. It embodies an economic — rather than a formalistic — approach that reflects the overall pragmatism of the Bankruptcy Code.

7. The transfer must enable the creditor to receive more than it would have received in a liquidation if the transfer had not taken place (11 U.S.C. §547(b)(5)). This restriction is frequently referred to as requiring that the transfer have a preferential effect. If the creditor would have received the same payment in a Chapter 7 proceeding without the transfer, the distributional objectives of the Code are not violated by permitting the creditor to keep the transfer.

The circumstances under which a transfer permits a creditor to receive more than it would in liquidation are fairly simple: If a liquidation would yield anything less than payment in full of all claims, the transfer to an unsecured creditor always permits that creditor to receive more than it would have received in liquidation. The unsecured creditor reduces its claim dollar for dollar with the payment it receives. But the claim would be worth only some pro rata distribution in liquidation. Similarly, a payment to a partially secured creditor reduces the unsecured portion of the claim first, since the security interest remains in effect to cover the remainder of the debt. By definition, the undersecured creditor who receives a payment is also receiving more than it would have received in liquidation. Because the creditor holds the security interest until the debt is paid in full, on any undersecured debt, the unsecured portion is in effect paid off first.

The only creditor who does not improve its position from a pre-petition payment is the creditor who would have been paid in full in liquidation — the fully secured creditor. Payment to a creditor with a valid security interest in collateral that meets or exceeds the creditor's claim does not constitute a preference when it is paid shortly before bankruptcy. Such a creditor would receive payment in full either way, with or without the disputed payment. To be sure, the secured creditor received the time value of the money and reduced its overall risk, but in the rough justice world of bankruptcy law, these benefits are overlooked. Only the debt, the value of the collateral, and the transfer received are subject to scrutiny.

* * *

Finally, it is worth noting what is not an element of voidable preference law. The Code contains no intent or state-of-mind provision. Transactions are set aside because of their effects, regardless of whether either the business or the creditor intended to create a preferential transfer. Moreover, the Code does not require that the transfer diminish the estate — although the concept seems to be related to the provision that the transfer be of "an interest of the debtor." Some creditors raise equitable arguments, trying to preserve certain transactions that they entered into in good faith or that they believe did not diminish the estate. The Code provisions render these arguments completely irrelevant.

Because the definition of voidable preferences turns on such highly technical provisions, the Code provides additional details to clarify when some transfers take place. Generally, transfers of security interests and mortgages take place when they are good against other creditors under applicable non-bankruptcy law (11 U.S.C. §547(e)(1)). A transfer of real property takes place when it is so perfected that a bona fide purchaser could not defeat the transferee's interest (11 U.S.C. §547(e)(1)(A)). Similarly, a transfer of an interest in personal property takes place when it is perfected (11 U.S.C. §547(e)(1)(B)). This means, in effect, that the filing to perfect these interests is itself a transfer.

Some leeway is inserted into the Code, however, to reflect the fact that a creditor may take a security interest and file it a few days later. The Code deems such a transfer to occur at the time it takes place between the debtor and the transferee, if the perfection step is taken within thirty days (11 U.S.C. §547(e)(2)). This gives a creditor thirty days to file its interest and still have its perfection declared contemporaneous with the rest of the transaction between the business and its creditor. Thus, the creditor who lends money in return for a security interest, which it perfects within thirty days, has not filed on account of an antecedent debt and hence is not subject to having the filing set aside. In the judgment of the Code drafters, these intervals conform with standard business practices, and the bankruptcy system protects them.

Sometimes the facts are reversed, so that the filing precedes the business's acquisition of property. This often occurs when the creditor has an after-acquired property clause, sweeping subsequent property into the creditor's net, or when the creditor has a floating lien, covering such property as inventory and accounts receivable where the identity of the particular pieces of collateral tend to change over time. In these situations, the Code deems the transfer to take place when the business acquires rights in the collateral (11 U.S.C. §547(e)(3)). This means that if the business acquires any property within the preference period before filing and the property is covered by any creditor's security interest, the transfer occurs when the business acquires rights in the property and the transaction is subject to voidable preference attack.

Exceptions to the Voidable Preference Rules

Some transactions are protected even though they may be preferential transfers. The exceptions are as specific as the rule creating preferences, however, and transactions that do not quite fit the exceptions can still be set aside.

The almost-contemporaneous exchange is protected (11 U.S.C. §547(c)(1)). A truly contemporaneous exchange, such as the transfer of goods for cash or the transfer of a loan for security interest, is not a voidable preference because there is no antecedent debt (11 U.S.C. §547(b)(2)). But a transaction may be intended by the parties to be a contemporaneous exchange for new value and be only substantially contemporaneous. If one examines a transaction closely, it might be that the seller gave the debtor goods just minutes before the debtor paid the creditor — technically making the payment on account of an antecedent debt. Once again proving their pragmatism, the Code drafters wanted to avoid such hyper-technicality, so they added an exception to make it clear that substantially contemporaneous exchanges could be saved as well. The exception reinforces the policy decisions evident in the antecedent debt provisions in the Code.

When the provision was adopted, a number of people thought it would apply to payment by check. If the business paid for goods with a check and the creditor cashed it in the ordinary course, the parties may well have intended this to be a contemporaneous exchange, although there was a brief extension of credit while the check was presented for payment and cleared. The Code protects such a transaction as substantially contemporaneous. But if the debtor post-dated the check, the parties would have intended a credit relationship, and the transaction would not qualify under the subsection 547(c)(1) exception, no matter how brief the period of credit extension. If the check was dishonored and paid only after it was presented a second time or after other collection efforts, the transaction would no longer be substantially contemporaneous and would lose its qualification for the exception as well. This interpretation has become somewhat controversial, however, and not all court decisions are consistent on the point.

Ordinary-course payments are also protected from set-aside as voidable preferences (11 U.S.C. §547(c)(2)). If a debt is incurred in the ordinary course of the business of the debtor and the creditor is repaid in the ordinary course of business according to ordinary business terms, the transaction will be protected. This exception insulates payments that did not result from the creditor's stepped-up collection efforts, thereby preserving ordinary commercial routines. Thus, only extraordinary activities of the pre-petition business and its creditors are monitored under the Code scheme. Of course, the exception permits the business to prefer some creditors "in the ordinary course," and its application may be broader than its policy justification. Like the provisions exempting cash transactions, this provision permits the business to remain in business even while it is in financial difficulty. Its creditors can continue ordinary operations and not be concerned that they will have to disgorge their payments if the business files for bankruptcy.

Purchase money security interests (PMSIs) are given special protection in bankruptcy (11 U.S.C. §547(c)(3)). A PMSI loan is used to purchase the property that becomes the collateral for a loan. So, for example, a business that buys a truck and gives a security interest in that truck has just agreed to a PMSI. A PMSI that is perfected within thirty days of the time the business receives possession of the collateral will be insulated from voidable preference attack (11 U.S.C. §547(c)(3)). The rationale is similar to the PMSI exception in Article 9 of the Uniform Commercial Code, following the theory that such lending should be encouraged because the estate is not diminished by such a transaction.

Creditors who extend subsequent unsecured credit after they have received a voidable preference can offset their later extensions against any obligation to disgorge the preferences (11 U.S.C. §547(c)(5)). Under the old Act, the courts used a "net result" test to determine the scope of this exception. This involved adding up all the credit extensions from the creditor and all the payments from the business within the ninety days before bankruptcy, regardless of the specific order for each. Only the final balance, if it favored the creditor, was a preference. The current Code exception gives more limited protection to creditors. The Code protects only subsequent extensions of credit. An extension of credit that precedes the voidable preference saves nothing, whereas an extension of credit that follows the preference will offset the preference. So, for example, if a business pays $1,000 to an unsecured supplier eighty days before bankruptcy, and the supplier sends another $1,200 in goods fifty days before bankruptcy, there is no recovery of the $1,000 voidable preference payment. But if the supplier sends $1,200 in goods eighty days before bankruptcy and receives a payment fifty days before bankruptcy, the payment is a voidable preference.

There is an equitable notion at work here: Creditors that have aided the estate after their preferences should get credit for their subsequent aid, but those who aided the business and then received transfers from the business are just like every other creditor who aided the business, so they should get no special help.

Inventory and accounts receivable financing are given special protection (11 U.S.C. §547(c)(5)). The high turnover of the items in inventory and receivables makes security interests on such items vulnerable to set-aside as voidable preferences. In a grocery store, for example, the canned goods for sale on June 1 are not likely to be exactly the same cans as those for sale on the following September 1, even if there are an equal number of cans of fruits and vegetables on both dates. Similarly, the accounts outstanding for a department store on June 1 are not likely to be exactly the same accounts with the same amounts owed three months later. All that new inventory and receivables that the business acquired in the ninety days preceding bankruptcy were subject to a lender's after-acquired property clause, making them subject to attack as voidable preferences in a later bankruptcy.

The Code protects security interests in such collateral, if they can meet a test. The difference between the value of the collateral and the outstanding loan is determined for two points in time, the date ninety days before the bankruptcy filing and again on bankruptcy filing day. If the loan was oversecured ninety days before filing, the security interest at filing is fully protected. If the loan was undersecured ninety days earlier, the portion of the security interest that reduces the undersecurity by bankruptcy day will be avoided (11 U.S.C. §547(c)(5)). This means, for example, that if the lender's inventory loan was undersecured by $50,000 on the ninetieth day before bankruptcy, but was undersecured by only $20,000 on bankruptcy day, the interest would be avoided on $30,000 of the collateral. The actual numbers of both the loan and the collateral value are immaterial, except to calculate the undersecurity. Only changes in undersecurity are relevant.

The inventory or accounts lender that was oversecured on the ninetieth day before bankruptcy can always increase its oversecurity during the time preceding the bankruptcy filing. This, of course, is the same rule that would be applicable to any other creditor oversecured on the ninetieth day before bankruptcy. Since the creditor can collect only the total outstanding amount of the loan, any increase in oversecurity is not technically an improvement in position. That view, of course, is the view of a lawyer and not of the businessperson who sweats out the shifts in collateral value while worrying about getting repaid.

While the oversecured lender is protected from a voidable preference attack, the Code exception does not protect the undersecured inventory or receivables financer that improves its position within the ninety days preceding bankruptcy. If, for example, an inventory lender was undersecured by $1 million on the ninetieth day before bankruptcy, a reduction of the deficit to $200,000 would result in a voidable preference of $800,000. The Code does, however, give the undersecured inventory or accounts lender a break by ignoring shifts in account balances and changes in the identity of the collateral during the course of the ninety day pre-bankruptcy period. The fact that the inventory lender may have been undersecured by $1.5 million on the forty-fifth day before bankruptcy is irrelevant; only the valuations and debts on the ninetieth day before bankruptcy and on bankruptcy day are relevant. This approach balances competing goals: It encourages inventory and receivables financing that would otherwise most likely be obliterated in bankruptcy, while it discourages the inventory and receivables lenders from eve-of-bankruptcy pressure on the business to run up collateral values to protect the creditor's bankruptcy position.

Finally, the 2005 amendments added another break for creditors who had received voidable preferences. In business cases, transfers with an aggregate value less than $5,475 cannot be set aside by the DIP. Creditors that had been stung by demands for small amounts that they had received in the ninety days preceding bankruptcy argued that they could not afford to go to some distant bankruptcy court to litigate over these small payments, even when they were not owed. So Congress gave them a break, saying they could keep these relatively modest preferences. Of course, Congress did not hear from all the creditors whose returns had been boosted from the recovery of preferences from other creditors, nor did they hear from the creditors who got better payments because the recovery of small amounts helped stabilize and refinance the business. This distortion highlights another systemic limitation in congressional policymaking.

Impact on Business Negotiations Outside Bankruptcy

If the Code permitted all pre-bankruptcy transactions to stand after the filing, creditors would be encouraged to start a feeding frenzy of pre-bankruptcy collection activities the instant companies were rumored to be in trouble. Quick, aggressive creditors would receive payment in full, whereas those who worked with the business and extended more unsecured credit would lose everything. The push by creditors might be enough to sink some businesses that otherwise could survive their economic crisis, thereby increasing the cost of economic stumbles by turning them into economic failures. Of course, some creditors may simply push the business earlier, but the business has control over the bankruptcy filing date. If a business has been subjected to aggressive collection efforts, the business can choose bankruptcy before the preference period has run and thus undo the transactions. By examining pre-bankruptcy collection efforts and by avoiding those collection efforts that permit a particular creditor to receive more than a pro rata distribution of the estate, the bankruptcy system reduces the creditors' incentive to act individually and aggressively when a business is in trouble. In doing so, the bankruptcy law exercises some restraint on the activities of creditors to dismantle ongoing businesses, to dissipate the value of the estate through piecemeal liquidation, and to push the business into bankruptcy.

Voidable preference law also influences negotiations between parties outside bankruptcy. If a creditor pushes too hard, the business can counter with a threat to file for bankruptcy and take back any benefits recently conveyed to that creditor. Because voidable preference law gives the business a valuable tool for setting aside transactions, that tool can be used effectively by the business trying to negotiate a successful reorganization outside bankruptcy.

Although it may be important to protect a failing company from being dismantled, such a policy will not enhance the value of failing companies generally if all transactions can subsequently be undone. Suppliers, for example, might conclude that it is unwise to engage in any transaction with a faltering company, even a cash sale, if the company could later reverse the transaction when it files for bankruptcy. This observation provides a balancing element to the preference set-aside provisions. Transactions that are useful to the business must be encouraged.

Voidable preference provisions and other devices that recover cash and assets for the estate have a practical impact on many reorganizations. Recovery of payments often provides a source of funding for the new reorganization effort. When security interests are set aside, the business is relieved of the obligation to provide adequate protection in order to keep using property during the reorganization. Moreover, the property that is now freed from a security interest may become collateral in post-petition refinancing. In addition, the ability of the business to recover voidable preferences may affect the willingness of various creditors to assist the DIP's reorganization effort. Creditors who thought they were paid in full now find they are pro rata participants in the reorganization effort and that their best prospect for payment in full is to cooperate in the reorganization effort.

STATUTORY LIENS

Sometimes a creditor enjoys an enhanced position not by its own actions to collect a payment or to negotiate for a security interest, but by virtue of state law provisions that give it preferential treatment. Such grants of priority repayment rights from state law are grouped together under the rubric of statutory liens. The extent to which the bankruptcy system recognizes such state law preferences will determine whether those creditors receive better treatment in bankruptcy than the general creditors do.

Basic Structure

Not all liens imposed by state law are voided in bankruptcy. Instead, the Code focuses on certain disfavored liens that are likely to be invoked only in the bankruptcy process. The DIP has the power to set aside liens that first become effective when the business files for bankruptcy, becomes insolvent, suffers the appointment of a custodian or the initiation of insolvency proceedings, or fails to meet certain financial conditions (11 U.S.C. §545(1)). In addition, the DIP may set aside statutory liens that would not be enforceable against a bona fide purchaser (11 U.S.C. §545(2)). Landlords' liens for rent are also set aside (11 U.S.C. §545(3)).

Statutory liens vary from state to state. Some states protect suppliers and independent contractors in the construction industry. Others protect those who provide services on personal property, such as car mechanics, watch repairmen, and dry cleaners. Personal injury victims get liens in some states, and attorneys benefit from charging liens that protect the proceeds of successful litigation. If these liens are generally applicable — that is, if they apply to businesses that are both solvent and insolvent, in bankruptcy and out of bankruptcy — then they are usually respected. Only the liens of a kind enumerated in Section 545 — mostly those that become effective only when the business is in financial trouble or landlord's liens — are voided, while all other liens are preserved.

One lien that is triggered by insolvency has deliberately been preserved in the Code scheme and expanded in the 2005 amendments. Goods suppliers have long enjoyed a special preference under the U.C.C.: the right of reclamation (U.C.C. §2-702). With some limitations, this right permits the seller to get back the goods it had sold to a buyer who turned out to be insolvent. Of course, the seller could have protected itself with a perfected purchase money security interest, but the reclamation right gave the seller similar protection even though it had never obtained (nor recorded) a security interest in the goods it shipped. This reclamation right was recognized in bankruptcy, but the Code severely limited that right. Because the right to reclaim amounted to the same kind of preference over other creditors as a security interest without having satisfied the Article 9 requirements of consent, notice, and filing, the Bankruptcy Code sharply limited the time available to exercise the right to reclaim the shipped goods.

In 2005, Congress gave suppliers of goods a greatly expanded right of reclamation. Under Section 546(c), if the debtor receives the goods while insolvent and within forty-five days of filing for bankruptcy, the seller may have a right to get the goods back if it makes a timely written demand. In addition, a seller of goods received by the debtor within the last twenty days before bankruptcy gets an automatic administrative priority, a right to a 100 percent payment for those goods rather than the pro rata distribution available to all the other unsecured creditors (11 U.S.C. §503(b)(9)).

These two provisions represent a great deal of leverage for this class of creditors. They also increase the business's need for cash at the very start of the case (to pay the suppliers immediately or to replace the reclaimed goods to keep the business running). The changes also add still more confusion to the maelstrom typical of a new Chapter 11 case because of the potential administrative chaos in determining which suppliers are entitled to which goods. Correspondingly, this increased preference for the suppliers of goods may operate to the prejudice of other creditors, such as the suppliers of services who will have to await payment from a now-diminished pool. The provision also increases the risk that fewer companies will be able to reorganize successfully, an outcome that can injure everyone who depends on that reorganization, from a taxing authority to a retired employee. Here, as elsewhere in bankruptcy, is a reminder that a benefit to one creditor often comes out of the pockets of other creditors who may be even less able to withstand the losses.

Summary

The DIP may set aside improvements in creditor positions on the eve of bankruptcy. The provisions on voidable preferences and those on statutory liens work together to permit the DIP to avoid both the special deals the parties negotiated shortly before filing and the special deals the legislature granted to certain creditors. By recovering these benefits for the estate, the debtor forces these creditors to share pro rata in its failure.

FRAUDULENT CONVEYANCES

Fraudulent conveyance law was first introduced into debtor-creditor law with the passage of the Statute of Elizabeth in 1571. The statute was designed to prevent debtors in distress from conveying away their property to keep it beyond the reach of their creditors. American jurisdictions adopted fraudulent conveyance law, either by statute or by incorporation into the common law. During the eighteenth and nineteenth centuries, case law became somewhat confused and contradictory. In 1918, the National Conference of Commissioners on Uniform Laws adopted a uniform act that was subsequently adopted in twenty-four states and that influenced the variations used in the other states. In 1984, the Conference redrafted the fraudulent conveyance provisions, proposing a new Uniform Fraudulent Transfer Act that was adopted in most states. States that did not adopt the uniform law adopted somewhat similar provisions either by statute or by common law. Today, bankruptcy law incorporates state fraudulent conveyance law and provides for a federal fraudulent conveyance law in bankruptcy as well.

Basic Structure

The Code incorporates fraudulent conveyance law into its structure by giving the DIP two alternatives: The DIP can exercise all the state-law recovery rights of unsecured creditors, or it can use a federal fraudulent conveyance law (11 U.S.C. §§544(b), 548). This double-barreled attack on fraudulent conveyances permits the DIP to use the laws that favor the surest recovery. For example, the Uniform Fraudulent Transfer Act gives creditors — and hence the DIP — four years to bring an action after a transfer (UFTA §9). This would obviously permit recovery in some cases that would be missed under the two-year statute of limitations in the federal law (11 U.S.C. §548(a)). Moreover, the UFTA creates an alternative one-year statute of limitations that begins to run only when the transfer "was or could reasonably have been discovered by the claimant," which is not available in the federal statute (UFTA §9(a)).

In addition, federal fraudulent conveyance law carries some benefits not found in state law. Many state laws, for example, permit only existing creditors to sue in constructive fraud cases, whereas the federal provisions permit the DIP to sue even if no creditor was owed an obligation at the time the fraudulent transfer occurred. The DIP can choose how it will proceed. It gets the maximum recovery, measured by whatever the creditors collectively could have gotten at state law or the rights granted to the estate under the Bankruptcy Code.

Federal fraudulent conveyance law covers two kinds of potentially fraudulent transfers. If the DIP can show that the debtor had "actual intent to hinder, delay, or defraud" existing or future creditors by making the transfer, the DIP can set the transfer aside (11 U.S.C. §548(a)(1)(A)). Historically, fraudulent conveyance law turned on whether the debtor had engaged in certain transactions that had "badges of fraud." The enumerated badges grew through the years, but so did the creativity of businesses that made transfers to escape paying their creditors. The Code now uses an actual-intent standard, which does not require any particular element or badge of fraud. Although the test is subjective, "actual" intent is not quite "actual," that is, it may be inferred from the behavior of the debtor. If such intent is proven to the satisfaction of the court, then the transfer is a fraud on the creditors, and the DIP is entitled to set it aside.

Federal fraudulent conveyance law covers all transfers by a debtor within two years of the bankruptcy filing (11 U.S.C. §548(a)). Once again, transfers are defined broadly to include a wide range of activities (11 U.S.C. §101(54)). The fraudulent conveyance provision reiterates that both voluntary and involuntary transfers are within the ambit of this provision.

The second kind of fraudulent transfer in the federal system is a transfer that is constructively fraudulent. These transactions require no showing of the debtor's intent. The Code provides that a transfer is fraudulent if the debtor receives less than a reasonably equivalent value in exchange for the transfer, if the business was insolvent at the time of the transfer (11 U.S.C. §548(a)(1)(B)). Reasonably equivalent value (called REV among professionals) is like "actual intent" in that the standard is heavily fact-specific. Paying off an antecedent debt constitutes receipt of reasonable value (forgiveness of an equivalent amount of debt), although such payments may trigger scrutiny under the voidable preference laws (11 U.S.C. §§548(d)(2)(A), 547(b)).

The critical question in most litigation on this issue is whether the business received reasonably equivalent value for the transfer. Sometimes it is a simple case of selling an item at a price that is too low. If, for example, an insolvent business sells a piece of machinery valued at $10,000 for $100, the transaction is probably not for REV. Where is the less-than-reasonable price point? At some point, the sale becomes a constructive fraud on the creditors, but no one is quite sure in advance where that point is.

Alternatively, sometimes the difficulty is that the non-debtor party to the transaction gave adequate consideration, but the consideration went to someone other than the debtor business. If, for example, an insolvent subsidiary business guaranteed a loan to a parent corporation but all the loan proceeds went only to the parent, the subsidiary would not have received REV for its guarantee. The guarantee contract would be enforceable under contract law, but it could be set aside in bankruptcy if the other elements of fraudulent conveyance law were met.

The DIP must also show that the debtor was insolvent at the time of the transaction or became insolvent as a result of the transfer (11 U.S.C. §548(a)(1)(B)(ii)(I)). The insolvency provisions in fraudulent conveyance law take a number of forms. The Code defines insolvency using a balance-sheet test, exclusive of any property transferred with intent to hinder, delay, or defraud (11 U.S.C. §101(32)(A)(i)).

In addition, if the business is left with "unreasonably small capital" after the transaction, the conveyance can be deemed fraudulent (11 U.S.C. §548(a)(1)(B)(ii)(II)). Finally, if the business believed it would incur debts that would be beyond its ability to repay as the debts matured, the conveyance could be set aside (11 U.S.C. §548(a)(1)(B)(ii)(III)). By using multiple approaches to define the company's financial health at the time of the transfer, the Bankruptcy Code preserves maximum flexibility for the DIP to set aside transactions when the transactions took place while the company was ailing and the transactions injured the estate.

A transfer for less than reasonably equivalent value when the debtor was insolvent can be set aside by the DIP under federal fraudulent conveyance law without any showing that the creditors in bankruptcy are in fact the same creditors as those existing at the time of the transfer. This differs from a state-law fraudulent conveyance action, which typically requires that the action be brought by a creditor existing at the time of the transfer, if the action is based on constructive fraud. This illustrates once again the broad reach of the powers the DIP is given in order to protect all the creditors in bankruptcy — not just the subset that can prove specific harm pre-bankruptcy.

Similarly, the Code protects creditors from businesses that might shift assets to insiders rather than make them available to those who are owed money (11 U.S.C. §548(a)(1)(B)(ii)(IV).

This provision covers transfers for the benefit of insiders or obligations such as employment contracts that are signed with insiders if the business was insolvent and it received less than reasonably equivalent value.

Finally, the Code includes some protection for the transferee who now faces giving back property or money to the bankrupt business. If the transferee acts in good faith, it is given a lien against the property transferred to the extent it had given value for it (11 U.S.C. §548(c)). To revisit an earlier example, if a buyer paid $100 for equipment worth $10,000, it might be required to give back the equipment (or its value, if the equipment is gone), but the buyer could insist that the company refund its $100. In effect, the deal is undone. This is not the great deal the buyer thought it was getting, but it is better than losing everything. This completes the balancing of interests between the transferee and the creditors and attempts to make the transferee whole.

The most powerful — and controversial — application of fraudulent conveyance law has followed in the wake of leveraged buyouts (LBOs) that have crashed into bankruptcy. In a typical LBO, the buyers of a target business offer the shareholders money for all the outstanding shares. The money comes from a lender, who takes a security interest in the shares of the business. So far, so good. But when the sale is consummated, by pre-arrangement the buyers commit the business to repay the debts and cause the target business to execute a security interest in all the business's unencumbered assets to secure the loan used to buy the business. This creates new owners of the business who have invested very little (hence the term leveraged). It also leaves the target business with huge debt obligations and virtually no unencumbered assets. After the transaction, if the business cannot meet its obligations, it goes into bankruptcy. If the security interest is valid, only the secured creditors (the financers of the purchase of the business) will be likely to see any recovery.

Some courts have permitted the DIP to use fraudulent conveyance law to set aside the security interests in all the business's unencumbered property and to avoid the promises to pay on the LBO loans. They reason that the debtor business received nothing for its promise to pay and its security interest, making the transaction a classic fraudulent conveyance. Other courts permit the set-aside on alternative fraudulent conveyance grounds, ruling that the parties to the LBO had actual intent to hinder, delay, or defraud outstanding creditors.

The various forms that LBOs may take are limited only by the imagination of investment bankers and eager investors. In some fact settings, courts have found that the elements of a fraudulent conveyance have not been proven. Moreover, some courts have found that the transaction can be undone with respect to some parties, such as the financer, but not others, such as the buyer who did not understand the leveraged nature of the financing purchase.

Summary

One of the oldest debtor-creditor provisions in our legal system is incorporated into the Code twice. Creditors can use state law, incorporated through the Bankruptcy Code, or federal law, directly provided in the bankruptcy law, to unwind fraudulent transactions. A sale or other conveyance may be fraudulent if it is made with intent to injure the creditors or if it transfers something of value without a reasonably fair exchange. Property pulled back into the estate by a fraudulent conveyance action is used to enhance the value of the estate and to benefit the creditors collectively. Like other avoidance provisions, fraudulent conveyance actions are frequently used to provide funding for the reorganization effort.

Fraudulent conveyance law creates the baseline of rules for debtor behavior. Even when the creditors negotiated for no special deal, the insolvent debtor is obligated not to act to injure its creditors. By curbing transfers made with intent to hinder, delay, or defraud, the law once again denies the debtor the opportunity to hide money from creditors or favor outsiders over the creditors. This provision thereby enhances the equality of treatment among creditors that is prized by the Code. When the debtor has no intent to injure the creditors with its pre-filing transfers, fraudulent conveyance law serves a somewhat different function. By restricting certain transfers that do not return fair consideration to the estate, the law provides some control over distress sales and piecemeal liquidations that dissipate the value of the estate. Fraudulent conveyance law makes some deals with faltering companies just too good to be true. Deals with insolvent businesses for very low consideration can be set aside by the debtor's other creditors.

STATE AVOIDANCE LAWS

In addition to state fraudulent conveyance laws, other state statutes give creditors rights to recover certain transfers of the debtor. State corporation laws, for example, may provide that creditors may set aside a company's dividends if they were paid from any source other than retained earnings. The DIP, acting on behalf of the creditors, is able to enforce those state-law rights.

General Operation

The Code provides that the DIP may avoid any transfer of an interest of the debtor that can be avoided at state law by an unsecured creditor (11 U.S.C. §544(b)). By limiting the application to rights given unsecured creditors, the Code permits recovery only of collective rights.

The primary use of section 544(b) is to incorporate state fraudulent conveyance law into the federal scheme, which was discussed earlier. But the provision is not limited to enforcement of such laws. State restrictions on declarations of dividends or on usurpation of corporate opportunities, for example, may be used by the DIP to recover assets in bankruptcy. Similarly, in appropriate circumstances, the DIP may use state bulk sales laws to recover assets on behalf of the creditors.

In proving the elements of the state-law creditors' claim, the status of the DIP is not hypothetical, as it was with the strong-arm clause (11 U.S.C. §544(a), (b)). This means that the DIP must meet every requirement of the state-law action or represent a creditor that meets the qualifications. If, for example, state law provides that only creditors existing at the time of a challenged transaction can enforce these state-granted rights, the DIP must find such a creditor among the estate's creditors. If no creditor qualifies, the DIP has no case.

If the DIP finds such a creditor, however, the DIP can act on behalf of the estate to set aside the entire transaction, effectively accomplishing much more than any individual creditor might have done outside bankruptcy. This principle, obliquely articulated in *Moore v. Bay*, was incorporated into the bankruptcy system both by legislative history and by subsequent case law. If, for example, the DIP can find one qualifying creditor that was owed one dollar, the DIP can set aside a $10 million transaction. Moreover, when the DIP recovers, it does so on behalf of all the creditors. The $10 million will be divided pro rata among all the claims against the estate. Once again, the DIP has collection rights rooted in state law, but the rights are enhanced when they are exercised on behalf of all the creditors in bankruptcy.

Summary

The DIP succeeds to the collective rights of all the creditors to enhance the estate and equalize the distribution of estate assets. In general, the DIP has the same rights and must meet the same burdens as a creditor suing in state court. But once a DIP can set aside a transaction, it can recover all the benefit of the avoided transaction, not just the benefit that could have been recovered by the complaining creditor. This gives the DIP collective rights better than those of the creditors.

EQUITABLE SUBORDINATION

Even if a creditor does not run afoul of any of the specific provisions that could cause a transfer to be set aside, it may still face a problem in bankruptcy. If the creditor has acted "inequitably," it may find that its otherwise-valid security interest is lost or that its unsecured claim in bankruptcy is subordinated to the claims of all the other creditors. Conduct can be deemed inequitable if the creditor behaved in a way to injure the debtor business and, in turn, to injure other creditors. In such cases, the bankruptcy court may equitably subordinate the creditor's claims.

Operational Details

Equitable subordination is a common-law principle that establishes the baseline relationships in debtor-creditor law. The Code ratifies the judicial concept announced in *Pepper v. Litton* (11 U.S.C. §510(c)). The bankruptcy court has the power to subordinate a claim or to preserve a creditor's lien for the benefit of the estate (11 U.S.C. §510(c)). The court is instructed to use "principles of equitable subordination" (11 U.S.C. §510(c)).

Creditors generally specify collection rights against a debtor, but few creditors specify the underlying conditions for running the business. Corporations are to be run to profit the corporate entity, not some third party. Corporate law generally holds that creditors shall be paid ahead of equity holders.[5] If those principles are violated, the corporate officers may be liable.[6] If a creditor participates in activities that violate those principles, the creditor will be subject to subordinated treatment if the company files for bankruptcy. Like voidable preference and fraudulent conveyance laws, provisions for equitable subordination reduce the value of the insider position or the leverage some creditors may exercise to improve their position.

One kind of activity that is generally covered by subordination is that of an owner hoping to benefit from claiming creditor status. The owner may have operated the business with no capital investment, characterizing the owner's initial contributions as "loans" to the business, often secured by business property. If the business fails, debt holder are paid ahead of equity, and the owner hopes to line up ahead of other debtors to get its money back first (11 U.S.C. §1129(b)(2)). If the business tumbles into bankruptcy, even if the owner has fully and accurately documented the transaction, the court may subordinate the "debt" of the owner and treat it like equity—with payment at the end of the line.

Owners can, of course, lend money to their businesses, taking both equity and debt positions. But at some level of greed the owners risk too little of their own money as working capital, and the courts will treat their loans as equitably subordinated to the claims of the outside creditors.

Sometimes creditors who are outsiders take over the managerial role of the owner, and directly or indirectly exercise their power to divert assets to themselves. So, for example, a senior creditor might step in when the business is in trouble, begin running the operation and paying itself, even if it leaves the old owner nominally in control. When this exercise injures other creditors, particularly when it drains the estate of much-needed assets, the courts may determine that the outside creditors should be equitably subordinated to the other creditors of the estate.

The impact of equitable subordination is powerful. The effect of any demotion in priority of payment will usually be to deny any recovery at all to the creditor. Unless the estate has sufficient assets to pay all the other creditors in full, equitable subordination can mean that the creditor loses all possibility of recovery during the bankruptcy process.

In recent years, equitable subordination has begun to cover new ground. Leveraged buyouts have left debtor businesses burdened with more debt than they can possibly meet while all their assets have been locked up in security agreements in favor of those involved in the buyouts. When these LBOs have pushed companies into bankruptcy, the loan arrangements have sometimes become the subject of subordination actions. Moreover, the kinds of creditor behavior that have led to lender-liability actions outside bankruptcy are also covered by equitable subordination if the business goes bankrupt. Claims that the creditor has unreasonably cut off a line of credit and thereby caused the business to fail may give a court a reason to subordinate the lender's debt. The doctrine seems to be covering a wider variety of cases as parties create new ways to put their collection rights ahead of those of other creditors.

In determining whether a creditor's interests should be equitably subordinated, some courts examine whether the debtor business promised the creditor the right to exercise such control or to call a loan without notice. Whether the business agreed to such behavior is only part of the inquiry. An inquiry into the relationship between the pre-bankruptcy business and this creditor is a starting point, but bankruptcy is a collective proceeding that implicates the rights of all the creditors as well. Equitable subordination is about injury to the other creditors stemming from a violation of principles of corporate management. The debtor's willingness to give up rights to a single creditor should provide no insulation if the creditor has behaved inequitably vis-à-vis other creditors. By forcing creditors to give up security interests and other advantages that they extracted from troubled debtors, equitable subordination serves to enhance the wealth of the estate. Similarly, by reducing the number of general claimants and forcing some creditors to wait for collection until the general creditors have been paid, equitable subordination enhances the estate for the benefit of the general creditors.

The provisions on equitable subordination pose a jurisprudential issue that crops up throughout the bankruptcy system: To what extent should the provisions of the Code mandate its requirements, giving clear guidance to the parties and the courts, and to what extent should the Code authorize the courts to apply loosely articulated general principles of equity to counter the effects of unanticipated or unarticulated wrongs? Following hard on the heels of fraudulent conveyances, strong-arm statutes, and voidable preferences, the equitable subordination provisions seem to be the final, catch-all weapon in the DIP's arsenal.

The use of general equitable principles in the Code may simply be a call for the development of a common law to fill in the necessary details.[7] A series of cases, grounded in specific facts and articulating relevant principles, may guide future parties and ultimately inject predictability into the law. Nonetheless, the power given to the bankruptcy courts remains open-ended, designed to deal with new wrongs not covered by either current principles or applications. Unpredictability reigns, but the creative creditor can be hemmed in as quickly as it figures out new approaches to diminish the estate. Once again, the Code balances the advantages of certainty against the need for flexibility and responsiveness.

The indeterminacy of the boundaries of equitable subordination is dwarfed by an even broader provision of the Bankruptcy Code. According to Section 105, a bankruptcy court "may issue any order, process, or judgment that is necessary or appropriate to carry out the provisions of this title."

This broad grant of equitable power is characteristic of the design of the Code: Specific rules governing collection rights following a bankruptcy filing are coupled with a nonspecific grant of whatever power is necessary to effectuate the Code's provisions. The specific rules are in place to provide certainty, to encourage parties to plan their affairs in advance, and to reduce litigation and enhance settlement. The rules strike an explicit balance between the rights of the estate and the rights of individual creditors. But the Code also acknowledges that the rules will not cover all the circumstances of every failure. The residual grant of power is broad so that the court can provide protection in unanticipated circumstances to assist in the resuscitation of a failing business.

Courts are reluctant to use such unrestricted grants of power to rewrite bankruptcy obligations, however, and the statutory injunction that the court should use its power "to carry out the provisions of this title" creates difficult jurisprudential problems. The provision gives the bankruptcy courts the opportunity to make case-by-case decisions to effectuate the larger principles of the Code. At the same time, it forces the courts to confront the question of when the opportunity becomes an obligation, and how far afield they should range in finding protection for bankrupt debtors.

Equitable subordination may free assets for the reorganization effort by avoiding security interests that encumber the debtor's property. Subordination will also reduce the number of creditors that must be satisfied during the distribution. The court may also limit the subordinated creditor's right to vote on plan confirmation. Not surprisingly, threats to subordinate debt form a significant part of the negotiations of many Chapter 11 reorganizations.

If the court finds that appropriate grounds exist, the DIP has yet another device to reshape the estate: subordination of some creditors' interests. Subordination may involve losing a priority repayment status, such as forgoing a security interest and consequently participating merely as a general, unsecured creditor. Or subordination may result in a creditor's demotion to receipt of payment only after all other creditors have been paid, which frequently means no repayment at all. In either case, assets of the estate are redistributed from the subordinated creditor to all the other creditors.

POLICY CONSIDERATIONS

The tools available to reshape the operations and balance sheet of a business in Chapter 11 are extraordinary. These powers are virtually unknown outside bankruptcy. In the right circumstances, these tools can be used to resuscitate a business that appeared dead. They can also be used to reclaim assets from aggressive creditors and to reshape business operations, continuing and even expanding profitable work while shuttering unprofitable undertakings. The twin goals of preserving value and distributing that value according to a predetermined priority scheme are advanced with each of these tools.

Like anyone running a business, the DIP has the power to assume, assign, and reject contracts that are not yet completed. The difference is that the DIP can pick and choose among profitable and unprofitable contracts, and when it rejects an unprofitable contract, the other party to the contract is stuck like all other pre-petition creditors, hoping for a pro rata payment on the damage claim. Moreover, clauses that permit the other party to escape from a contract when the business begins to stumble financially are voided in bankruptcy.

Management of a failing business loses the opportunity to make promises to favor some friends by promising performance on losing contracts. The executory contract provisions put all the unperformed contracts on an even footing, with the decisions about which to preserve and which to breach governed only by the best interests of the estate. The provisions also prevent the other party to the contract from getting a windfall when the debtor business declares bankruptcy; if the DIP assumes, the other party must continue to perform.

With the executory contract provisions, the DIP has the power to reshape the operations of the business. This can be an extremely important tool in breathing life back into a failing business, enhancing recovery for all the creditors — including those with breach-of-contract actions.

The DIP can also transform the business balance sheet. The Bankruptcy Code gives the DIP the power to set aside both certain transfers to creditors that occur within ninety days before the bankruptcy filing and certain transfers to insiders that occur within a year before the filing. Avoiding these pre-bankruptcy collection efforts equalizes the distribution among creditors over a longer period of time. Outside bankruptcy, a creditor could keep whatever it could squeeze out of a debtor. In bankruptcy, by contrast, voidable preference law has the effect of treating all unsecured creditors alike, whether they have received payments shortly before bankruptcy or not. Voidable preference laws also reduce the power of old management to choose the creditors that get paid and the ones that do not. The DIP is obligated to enhance the estate, and voidable preference law is the tool to bring assets back for a fairer distribution.

The distributional consequences of recognizing state law statutory liens are similarly clear: Such liens are designed by state legislatures to prefer one group of creditors over another, moving the benefited creditors to the front of any collection line. To the extent that these liens are voided, the goal of equality among creditors is enhanced.

Why aren't all statutory liens voided? Some liens may be sufficiently a part of commerce that the drafters of the Code did not want to disturb their use. Moreover, the original passage of a number of statutory liens was justified on the grounds that the liens protected creditors that were unable to get security interests for one reason or another, suggesting that the statutory lien operates as a de facto security interest for these creditors. Liens that apply at all times and in all circumstances will be honored in bankruptcy. But a lien that is triggered by the insolvency of the business or by the business's filing a bankruptcy petition poses a threat to the uniformity and supremacy of the Bankruptcy Code. State laws providing for such liens are usually an obvious attempt by the local legislatures to determine the priority of repayment in the bankruptcy system. These liens are denied an effect in bankruptcy so that the distributional scheme of federal bankruptcy law triumphs over varying state distribution systems.

Fraudulent transfer law is a powerful tool in bankruptcy. It restricts the right of the insolvent debtor to injure creditors by conveying value from the business. Once a business files for bankruptcy, the DIP succeeds to the collective rights of the creditors, including the right to set aside fraudulent conveyances. By avoiding transactions in which management demonstrated an intent to hinder, delay, or defraud their creditors, the law polices businesses that seek to avoid repaying their creditors by hiding assets and making themselves appear insolvent. Although very little debtor-creditor law turns on the intent of the parties, this intent provision is a central element of the ability to monitor the behavior of debtors.

Fraudulent conveyance law also permits creditors — and, by extension, the DIP — to recapture property that has been transferred for less than fair consideration, even if no improper intent is suggested. By setting aside the transfers that dissipated assets without yielding equivalent value for the business, the DIP enlarges the estate and increases the chances that the business can survive and pay more to the creditors. Also, by scrutinizing transactions that occurred one or more years before filing, fraudulent conveyance law is another device for monitoring the behavior of all troubled debtors and making certain that some creditors have not been preferred ahead of others.

Equitable subordination provides a final, open-ended opportunity for the estate to avoid the impact of advantageous treatment that an individual creditor has managed to obtain. That creditor may lose a security interest, disgorge some other benefit, or be forced to stand in line behind other creditors. Whatever remedy the court ultimately orders, equitable subordination promotes equality of distribution among the creditors and provides one more tool to help the business survive.

All of these provisions — voidable preference, fraudulent conveyance, review of statutory liens, and equitable subordination — enhance the collective estate at a cost to an individual creditor. Each also has the effect of setting aside whatever intent the pre-bankruptcy management may have had to prefer friends or insiders, unraveling any attempt within a defined period to dissipate the value of the business by conveying it away.

CONCLUSION

The bankruptcy system gives the DIP wide latitude to reshape the debtor business. The DIP can pick among the business's obligations, choosing which contracts will become contractual obligations of the newly formed bankruptcy estate and which will become only claims for pro rata repayment. The DIP can also review the activities of the pre-petition debtor to determine whether payments of outstanding debts and assets that the debtor conveyed away should be recovered for the use of the estate. Sometimes valuable property and rights are drawn back into the estate, particularly when the estate assumes profitable contracts or recovers fraudulent conveyances or voidable preferences. At other times, individual creditors lose their priority collection rights, resulting in lower (or no) payments and diminished leverage to affect the course of the bankruptcy. As the estate grows after the initial filing, the DIP either has greater assets for distribution to the creditors collectively or has a better opportunity to create a viable business — or both.

~ 5 ~

Confirming the Chapter 11 Plan

The front door to Chapter 11 is wide — there are few restrictions on filing. But the back door is narrow — only about a third of all businesses that file for Chapter 11 manage to emerge with a confirmed plan of reorganization.[1]

For the businesses that do not confirm a plan, the problems are many. Often the business cannot generate an adequate cash flow to maintain its operations, and it simply collapses. In other cases, the death knell for the business is sounded when a secured creditor succeeds in lifting the automatic stay and repossesses property critical to the operation of the business. In some cases, failure to secure post-petition financing or an inability to settle a labor dispute will force the business to close. Even companies that confirm a reorganization plan may have liquidated large parts of the company to generate cash, so that the surviving business may be little more than a shadow of its pre-filing self.

For the businesses that make it to the plan-confirmation process, the overwhelming majority of those that confirm a plan do so with the consent of their creditors.[2] If all the creditors consent, there are few restrictions on the shape the plan may take. The Code provides for confirmation over the objection of the creditors in limited circumstances; however, few debtors actually litigate and successfully confirm a plan over the vigorous opposition of their creditors.

The provisions for plan confirmation are central to the Chapter 11 process. Confirmation is the final settlement of the rights of the parties. After the opening moments of a Chapter 11 filing, every negotiation with every creditor takes place with sharp awareness of what the creditors can and cannot legally demand in a plan confirmation. While the parties may decide to deviate from the Code provisions for other business reasons, plan confirmation requirements set the baseline requirements.

Sometimes the difficulties facing a business will manifest themselves long before a confirmation hearing. If a creditor can demonstrate that the business has little likelihood of meeting the Chapter 11 plan requirements, the creditor can derail the Chapter 11 case much earlier in the process and the business can be liquidated. For example, a creditor may file a motion to lift the automatic stay within minutes after the petition is filed. If the creditor can demonstrate that the debtor has no equity in the collateral and the debtor is unable to prove that it has a reasonable prospect for an "effective reorganization," the Chapter 11 proceeding may be over before it starts (11 U.S.C. §362(d)(2)). In effect, the court may hold an early mini-hearing to determine whether the debtor is likely to meet the plan-confirmation requirements later on.

The confirmation of a Chapter 11 plan completes the process begun at filing. When the Chapter 11 petition was filed, a new entity, the Chapter 11 estate, was created. If the Chapter 11 case is successfully concluded with the reorganization of the debtor, the estate will cease to exist and its assets will become those of the post-reorganization business. The new business will go on to operate without the continuing protections or burdens imposed by the Bankruptcy Code. The plan will, of course, reorder the relationship between the debtor and its creditors by discharging debt, reissuing stock, and so on. The plan may also call for some continuing protection of the debtor, such as a continuing injunction against certain creditor collection actions. But the automatic stay, the restrictions on post-petition operation, and other essential elements of Chapter 11 that have already been discussed will all cease at confirmation.

The plan-confirmation process sets the terms by which the bankruptcy estate will be converted to a post-reorganization business. Conceptually, when a plan is confirmed, the estate transfers its going-concern operation to the emerging post-reorganization business. The plan outlines the obligations of the emerging business, including the payout schedules and the discharge of debt of various classes of creditors. The plan also details the financing arrangements made for the proposed payouts and for the continuing operation of the business. In addition, the plan establishes the ownership of the new business. The owners may be new buyers, recently arrived on the scene. Or they may be the old owners of the business, who hope that their new efforts will be more successful. Or they may be the creditors of the old business, who take equitable ownership as part of the payback on their outstanding debts. All elements of the plan are open to negotiation — and dispute, if the parties cannot agree.

The rules of plan confirmation determine who may propose a plan, how the creditors may vote on plans, what happens to dissenting parties, and when plans can be confirmed without unanimous consent. These rules allocate negotiating power during the Chapter 11 process and guide the parties in shaping a consensual plan.

POWER TO PROPOSE THE PLAN

The power to propose a reorganization plan to be voted on by the creditors is widely perceived as a critical control element in the Chapter 11 negotiations. The party who can propose a plan has much control over both the shape of the post-reorganization business and the operation of the business in Chapter 11. To control the timing of the presentation of the plan is to control the progress of the Chapter 11 case. To propose the terms for the sale of the estate to the post-reorganization business and the final distribution of the assets is to have a profound influence on the outcome of the Chapter 11 process. The DIP wants exclusive power to propose a plan, whereas reluctant creditors may want to propose plans of their own. Creditor plans often require higher, quicker payouts or immediate liquidation of the business, particularly if the plan is proposed by a secured creditor who stands to lose little if the business is terminated.

BASIC STRUCTURE

Although every party in interest has an eventual right to propose a plan, companies that file for Chapter 11 get first crack (11 U.S.C. §1121(c)). The DIP is granted an exclusive period of time in which to propose and confirm a plan of reorganization. Section 1121(b) gives the debtor 120 days in which to propose its own plan of reorganization and Section 1121(c)(3) gives 180 days to solicit votes to confirm the plan. Both times are measured from the date of filing and overlap each other. During these times, no other party in interest can propose or solicit a different plan of reorganization.

The idea behind giving the DIP the first shot at proposing a plan is multileveled. Partly, it encourages management to file by assuring them that they will stay in the driver's seat for a period of time. Presumably management knows the most about the circumstances of the debtor's difficulties, and management may be best situated to propose a plan to solve them. Exclusivity also prevents a bankruptcy filing from turning into immediate chaos as different parties put forth their plans. By providing some stability and continuity, companies are spared a plunge into an immediate fight among multiple claimants. It also makes the company the central point for bringing together all the parties for negotiation.

In big reorganizations, those with thousands of outstanding contracts and leases, complex financial structures, and far-flung operations, 120 days of exclusivity was unlikely to provide the time needed to reorganize the business. Prior to the 2005 amendments, the courts had the power to extend exclusivity indefinitely. The courts might require a showing that the debtor was making good progress toward a plan and just needed more time to bring it together. Exclusivity might be extended because the debtor needed more time to sell off a division, to renegotiate contracts, or to settle a labor dispute. If a debtor could show that a recalcitrant creditor was the cause for delay, a court might further extend exclusivity. Whether — and how long — to extend exclusivity was entirely within the province of the bankruptcy court, and rarely overturned in any appeal. As a consequence, the discretion of the bankruptcy court figured heavily in the confirmation of big, complex Chapter 11 plans.

A second impact of exclusivity has been its effect on leverage in the great Chapter 11 negotiations. The possibility of languishing in bankruptcy month after month, with interest no longer running on the loan while the debtor remains protected by the automatic stay, brings many creditors to the bargaining table. They may not like it, but they are ready to take a haircut, get what they can, and move on. Sometimes the debtor who can credibly threaten to stay in Chapter 11 can herd the creditor cats into some semblance of a negotiated deal.

The 2005 amendments changed the dynamic. Now, no matter the reason for delay, no matter how complex the case or how outrageous the creditors' behavior, Section 1121(d)(2) imposes a cap on judicial discretion of eighteen months from the date of the filing to propose a plan and twenty months from the filing date to solicit votes. The debtor faces a firm deadline: Get your plan confirmed or face the possibility that every creditor in the case will propose less attractive alternatives.

The question of how long the DIP will have to control the case before the creditors can begin to propose their own plans has been hard fought at the policy level. If a creditor could propose a plan calling for a liquidation of the business at the inception of the case, the DIP would be put on the defensive quickly to prove it could come up with a more attractive payout scheme for the creditors. A DIP would likely make unwise promises on the business's behalf to stave off such attacks. At the same time, if the DIP could delay a plan proposal indefinitely while it operates comfortably in Chapter 11, pre-petition creditors would see the value of their claims sinking lower and lower and their willingness to agree to any repayment proposal rises. The hand that controls the plan proposal has great power in the Chapter 11 process.

If creditors could propose plans, particularly liquidation plans, from the instant of filing, there would be a risk that assets of the business would be dissipated. The value obtained from imposing an automatic stay on the creditors' collection of debts would be lost in many cases. The Chapter 11 debtor would spend a substantial portion of its resources fighting to survive before it had an opportunity to examine what could be accomplished to reshape the ongoing business. It would not have the opportunity to explore the implications of either the legal devices, such as assumption and assignment of executory contracts and avoiding preferential payments, or the business devices, such as dropping certain product lines and cutting back particular operations. In many cases, a period of exclusivity is necessary to protect the powers granted to the DIP elsewhere in the Code that enable the DIP to run the business for the benefit of the creditors.

At the same time, an unlimited period of exclusivity would not enhance the value of the estate if it permitted the DIP to run the business in Chapter 11 indefinitely. The creditor that can make a credible threat to propose a plan is better able to influence the DIP's operation of the business. If the DIP is wasting estate assets, the creditors can propose a liquidation plan. Alternatively, creditors may have different — and better — views about how the business can be structured to yield a better payout. When creditors can propose a plan, they are not put to the limited choice between voting yes and voting no on the DIP's plan. Instead, by proposing a plan, they can make asset-deployment judgments or reach going-concern values that the DIP might not develop. This permits the creditors to develop value-enhancing strategies for the debtor.

The ability to control the timing of a plan proposal has important distributional consequences as well. If a creditor that is likely to be paid in full, such as a fully secured creditor, could force the business into an early fight for its survival, the distributional consequences are obvious: The creditors with guaranteed repayments because of their interests in hard collateral could collect quickly and in full, and the other creditors would be paid less. If, instead, the DIP has unimpeded control over the reorganization process, other distributional consequences follow. The DIP management seeking to protect a future job and facing the likelihood of liquidation may offer only high-risk strategies that would reward the unsecured creditors if they paid off and consume the secured creditors' collateral if they did not.

For those who believe that debtors had too much running room before the 2005 amendments — or, more accurately, that bankruptcy judges were giving debtors too much running room by continuing to protect them with repeated extensions of exclusivity — the new, tighter deadlines are welcome. For those who believe that judges used extensions of exclusivity and the threat of lifting exclusivity to move cases along, this change seems quite wrong-headed. An uncooperative creditor can watch the calendar as closely as the debtor, knowing that if it can string the bankruptcy out for another few months, it can propose its own liquidating plan, grab what it can, and leave the debtor in ruins. Such a threat may cause a business to negotiate a reorganization package that appears to be more favorable to one creditor or to all the creditors, but that plan may be doomed to failure.

Either way, the 2005 statutory revisions are likely to have a powerful impact on cases — particularly the larger, more complex cases and the ones in which the food fights among the creditors were well underway by the time of the bankruptcy filing. The days when LTV Steel could take seven years to confirm a plan of reorganization are over. According to the data reported by Professor LoPucki (in http://lopucki.law.ucla.edu/corporations), the average time to confirm a plan for a big, publicly traded debtor has been 510 days, but the standard deviation is another 436 days — suggesting that some did it very quickly and a substantial number took a very, very long time. Whether the caps on judicial discretion to grant extensions in exclusivity will herald a new day of faster reorganizations or simply a time of really large liquidations is a question to be answered by the next round of empirical studies.

Even when every party is moving at maximum speed, delays occur. The business in Chapter 11 is typically fighting for its corporate life. Around the time the petition is filed, there is often a realignment of the debtor's business relationships. Frequently, trade credit is drying up and customers are turning skittish. The DIP may be in court to ask for approval to use cash collateral, and creditors may be demanding more information about the operation of the business and its long-term prospects. Employees may look for more secure jobs. Management's attention is divided between the legal details of operating a business in Chapter 11 and the business details of operating a business in serious trouble. Early conditions in most Chapter 11 cases are chaotic, so that keeping a business afloat during a reorganization proceeding is a challenging process.

Summary

The Code gives the DIP the exclusive right to file a reorganization plan during the first 120 days following the bankruptcy filing. If the plan is not accepted by 180 days into the proceeding, other parties may file their own plans. The court may extend the time limits by up to eighteen and twenty months respectively. Whenever the time period expires, the creditors have another opportunity to contest the control of the DIP and to monitor the DIP's proposed reorganization plans.

SPECIAL RULES FOR SMALL BUSINESSES

Although an Enron filing may dominate the headlines, far more small businesses than big businesses enter Chapter 11 each year. The data from the Business Bankruptcy Project show that the median business debtor in Chapter 11 had total liabilities of just $351,000.[3] Only 9.7 percent of the businesses in Chapter 11 had liabilities in excess of $5 million.[4] Unlike their shareholder-owned and investor-owned counterparts in the multimillion- or even billion-dollar range, it is likely that most of these small businesses are owner-operated. The resources available for attorneys' fees and accountants' reports make even the basic paper management different in small-business and large-business filings, although both are formally designated as business Chapter 11s and the same legal rules applied to both for many years.

The 2005 amendments created a new classification of debtor: the Small Business Debtor (11 U.S.C. §101(51D)). Every "person engaged in commercial or business activities" must take a close look to see if the regular rules of Chapter 11 apply or if this debtor will be further constrained by treatment as a small business debtor (11 U.S.C. §101(51D)(A)). Of course, the Bankruptcy Code defines a "person" to include partnerships and corporations (11 U.S.C. §101(41)).

Size can be measured in a number of ways. The Small Business Administration, for example, measures many businesses by the number of employees. For purposes of many public accommodation laws, landlords are measured by the number of rental units. Dow Jones reports classify companies by annual revenues. In bankruptcy, the measure of "small" is not by the size of the debtor, but by the size of the bills that are coming due. A small business debtor is one that "has aggregate noncontingent liquidated secured and unsecured debts as of the data of the petition . . . in an amount not more than $2,190,000"[5] (11 U.S.C. §101(51D)). Debts to insiders or affiliates are excluded from the total, probably to keep a strategic owner-operator from lending money to his own business on the eve of bankruptcy just to keep it out of the small business designation by going over the limit.

Why focus on the debts? They are certainly much easier to count than trying to figure out the value of the used typewriters and stock of paperclips in the business. Even so, debt presents it own tricky elements. The "noncontingent liquidated" debt concept has appeared before, showing up in the definition of eligibility for Chapter 13 (11 U.S.C. §109(e)). Its close cousin, "noncontingent undisputed" debt, appeared as the trigger for involuntary petitions (11 U.S.C. §303). Clearly Congress had some notion that counting the dollar value of the debts would be a fairly routine matter, and, for the majority of businesses with either huge debts or very modest debts, that is undoubtedly true. But, as in much of life, the margins can be tricky. An ordinary bank loan may be a noncontingent liquidated debt, but that status might change if the debtor plans to contest the amount owed.

For the small but well-advised debtor, the presence of a specific dollar amount of debt that will determine whether the debtor will be shuffled into a far more hostile Chapter 11 category is an invitation to engage in some pre-bankruptcy planning. The debtor who is somewhere under the magic

$2,190,000 can quit paying the utilities, stop making the promised pension plan contributions, and hit the company credit cards. That $2,190,000 number may be in a struggling debtor's mind as he or she decides that this might be a good time to buy a new truck, renovate the office, or take out a new line of credit.

The Code provides a single out to escape small-business treatment: If a creditors' committee is formed and it is active enough to satisfy the court that it can provide "effective oversight," then the even the tiniest business is no longer a "small business" (11 U.S.C. §101(51D)(A)). Once again, the opportunities for strategic behavior and cooperation with a few key creditors can significantly alter the application of this new set of rules.

The New Rules

In addition to the forms and disclosures required in all Chapter 11 cases, the small business debtor must attach additional information to its voluntary petition. Section 1116 requires management to append a balance sheet, statement of operations, cash flow statement, and federal income tax returns or file a statement, under penalty of perjury, that no such documents have been prepared. During the course of the bankruptcy, small business debtors will be required to file periodic financial and other reports containing information on the debtor's profitability and its projected cash receipts and disbursements (11 U.S.C. §308). The amendments also direct the Judicial Conference of the United States to prescribe standard form disclosure statements and plans of reorganization for small business debtors. Such forms are designed to be modified, so that small businesses will, at least in theory, have some capacity to modify the forms to fit their needs. These standardized forms may provide a degree of guidance to inexperienced lawyers and help creditors evaluate plans quickly.

The law is clearly moving small businesses toward a one-size-fits-all model.

In addition to the duties of TIBs or DIPs laid out in Sections 1106 and 1107, the small business debtor in Chapter 11 must add the duties in Section 1116. So, for example, management must attend meetings with the United States Trustee (§1116(2)). The debtor is specifically instructed to file all required schedules, file tax returns, and maintain insurance. While these are usually thought of as appropriate business practices for any debtor in Chapter 11, the point of spelling them out is to provide clearer grounds for dismissal of debtors who slip deadlines or can't assemble the paperwork.

Small business cases will also be subject to greater monitoring by the United States Trustee. The UST will be required to conduct an initial debtor interview "as soon as practicable" after filing (28 U.S.C. §586(a)(7)). The UST is instructed to investigate the debtor's viability, inquire about the debtor's business plan, explain the debtor's obligations to file monthly operating reports and other required reports, attempt to develop an agreed scheduling order, and inform the debtor of other obligations. The UST may also become a roving investigator, checking into the debtor's viability and making inquiries in the business community and visiting the debtor's business to "ascertain the state of the debtor's books and records, and verify that the debtor has filed its tax returns" (28 U.S.C. §586(a)(7)(B)). The UST is also charged with reviewing and monitoring the debtor's activities, to identify as promptly as possible "whether the debtor will be unable to confirm a plan." This represents a potentially important shift toward involving the UST in business operations as well as case administration.

Modified solicitation and disclosure rules also apply in small business cases (11 U.S.C. §1125(f)). The biggest change, however, is likely to come from the change in exclusivity rules. A small business debtor will have the exclusive right to propose a plan of reorganization for 180 days and the plan, whenever proposed, must be approved within 300 days of the bankruptcy filing or the case will be dismissed (11 U.S.C. §1121(e)). Courts may not extend those periods unless the debtor demonstrates that it is "more likely than not" that the court will confirm a plan within a reasonable period of time, a new deadline is imposed at the time the extension is granted, and an extension order is signed before the existing deadline has expired. The burden is on the moving party, usually the debtor, to show that it will propose a confirmable plan within a reasonable time period.

Targeting Small Businesses

The whole notion of a statute that singles out small businesses for heightened scrutiny has a somewhat otherworldly quality. There is no systematic evidence to suggest that small business bankruptcies are rife with fraud, abuse, or even heavy partying. Ironically, the general unsecured creditors who extend credit to these small debtors, represented by their trade group the Commercial Law League of America, vigorously opposed these changes, arguing that they would increase the leverage of the big banks and push more businesses into liquidation, leaving nothing for the trade debt, the suppliers and other smaller creditors. They lobbied against the bill but were unable to persuade Congress that the existing system was working all right in the small business cases.

The time limits imposed on plan confirmation have drawn particular fire. The available empirical evidence suggests that they are both too long and too short. That is, for the cases in which there is little hope of a reorganization, permitting the debtor to drift in Chapter 11 for six months (180 days) is wasteful and the statute does little to push these hopeless cases out faster than the judges were doing before the changes came into play. In a study focused on small business cases filed in Chicago in 1998, professors Douglas Baird and Edward Morrison determined that 91.5 percent of unsuccessful cases are resolved within 345 days of filing, the greatest number being resolved in the first two months. By contrast, successful cases took longer; more than a third of all the cases that eventually confirmed a plan of reorganization did so after 345 days. Data from the Business Bankruptcy Project indicate that in 2002 75 percent of all Chapter 11 cases were resolved in less than a year and 90 percent in less than eighteen months, but only about a third of the cases that were successful in confirming a plan were able to do so within nine months. Another 45 percent confirmed after eighteen months, making the addition nine months the key period for confirming cases. In short, the data suggest that the period of exclusivity — which has now been potentially extinguished by the amendments — is the most important zone of Chapter 11 success, as measured by plan confirmations.

The small business provisions raise yet another question: If the provisions here are good policy — more disclosures, limits on refiling — then why don't they apply to all businesses filing for bankruptcy? One possible explanation dates to the National Bankruptcy Review Commission, established by Congress in 1994 to review the bankruptcy laws and make recommendations for change. From the beginning, the commission was split into two camps, one that generally supported the bankruptcy system as it worked and one that was convinced that debtors of all stripes — business and consumer — were abusing their creditors.[6] To attack a wide range of problems, the commissioners decided to form working groups. The strongest critics of the debtors hoped to make substantial amendments to Chapter 11, but they ended up on the small business working group instead of the Chapter 11 working group. Big business lenders and the elite bankruptcy bar combined to persuade the commission that trying to make life tougher for debtors would not help anyone, but there was no strong constituency to speak on behalf of small businesses. The proposals from the commission's small business working group became the basis for the small business amendments that Congress ultimately adopted.[7]

PLAN PROCESS

Time limits and operations during a pending Chapter 11 may differ for large and small cases, but the basics of confirming a plan remain the same for everyone. Plans may be confirmed consensually, and parties may waive their rights in a reorganization if they determine that it is in their interests to do so. Even in a nonconsensual plan, some creditors may voluntarily waive their rights and support confirmation, giving the debtor the opportunity to confirm a plan over the objections of other creditors. It is not uncommon for a creditor to agree to less than full payment, based on its conclusion that partial payment in reorganization is likely to be better than partial or nonexistent payment in liquidation. Some creditors — particularly trade creditors, suppliers, and employees — may see the continuation of the business as being in their own long-term economic interests, and they may prefer to forgive old debts in order to continue working with a viable company. While parties may waive their rights, the delineation of these rights is nonetheless important because it stakes out each party's bargaining position and determines each party's leverage to halt confirmation of a reorganization plan.

Consensual Plans

Creditors are permitted to vote on reorganization plans. Once the creditors have consented, courts nearly always confirm the plan. Plans can be confirmed with less than full creditor approval. Chapter 11 sets out the process by which creditors vote on plans, and certain minimal protections are offered to dissenting creditors.

Plans deal with creditors by classes (11 U.S.C. §1122(a)). Each creditor is placed in a class with other creditors with substantially similar claims or interests (11 U.S.C. §1122(a)). Secured creditors have rights based on their collateral and their rights are strictly ordered: the first secured creditor on the property, followed by the second secured creditor on the same property, and so on for each piece of property that serves as collateral for a loan. As a result, each secured creditor's legal rights differ from those of all other creditors, including those of other secured creditors, so that each secured creditor is usually in a class by itself. Secured claims are bifurcated into their secured portions and unsecured portions. For example, a loan for $1 million that is secured by a piece of property worth $800,000, will be divided into a secured loan for $800,000 and an unsecured loan for the remaining $200,000 (11 U.S.C. §§502, 506 (a)).

Some claims, such as employees' wages and taxes, have no security, but they are given priority in collection. Whatever property remains after the secured creditors have realized on their collateral can be made available for the unsecured creditors, with the priority creditors at the head of the line. Priority claims are grouped with other claims of the same priority, so that, for example, all qualified employee wage claims are grouped together (an 11 U.S.C. §507(a)(4) priority).

Unsecured claims without priority are segregated from the secured and priority claims. Unsecured creditors are usually grouped together for pro rata treatment, although the plan may separate them into different classes (11 U.S.C. §1123 (a)(1)). Within each class, all creditors are treated alike (11 U.S.C. §1123 (a)(4)).

To confirm a plan, a plan proponent must submit a proposed disclosure statement and a proposed plan to the court for approval before circulating them to the creditors (11 U.S.C.

§1125(b)). The disclosure statement must contain adequate information about the business and the proposed plan for a "hypothetical reasonable investor" to make an informed judgment about the plan (11 U.S.C. §1125(a), (b)). The plan must specify the classes and the proposed treatment of each class, the disposition of assets, the recovery of estate assets, the assumption and rejection of executory contracts, settlements of various disputes, and the general plan for the business's operation (11 U.S.C. §1123(b)). The plan may provide for liquidation of the business (11 U.S.C. §1123(b)(4)). After the disclosure statement has been approved by the court, the plan and statement are circulated to all parties in interest. At that point, the creditors and shareholders vote on the plan (11 U.S.C. §1125(b)).

Voting Rights

Creditors vote by class. A class is deemed to have accepted a plan if creditors constituting more than one-half of the members of the class and representing at least two-thirds of the amount of debt owed to that class have voted in favor of the plan (11 U.S.C. §1126(c)). Voting must be "in good faith" (11 U.S.C. §1126(e)). A creditor's dissenting vote may not be counted, for example, if the plan proponent can prove that the creditor voted against the plan because it is a business competitor and is attempting to tie up the reorganization effort to cause the business to collapse. If the plan meets other Code restrictions set out below and if all classes accept the plan, the plan will be confirmed, notwithstanding the dissenting votes of a number of creditors within each class (11 U.S.C. §1129(a)(7), (8)).

Because of the importance of voting by classes, the DIP and the creditors often dispute the composition of the unsecured classes. The DIP would like to have unrestrained power to group creditors in a way that increases the likelihood that a majority in each class will consent to the plan it proposes. Alternatively, the DIP may hope to isolate the dissenting creditors for treatment in a nonconsensual plan. Not surprisingly, creditors reverse the strategy, arguing for the treatment that permits them to resist the DIP's classification efforts, calling them "gerrymandering." The creditors want groupings that increase their negotiating leverage.

The battle lines are clear, but the Code provides little guidance. A plan may designate a separate class of claims grouped together for administrative convenience (11 U.S.C. §1122(b)). In addition, creditors in the same class must have substantially similar interests (11 U.S.C. §1122(a)). But so long as those two points are met, the Code is otherwise silent. The latitude permitted the plan proponent to create separate classes of legally similar claimants continues to be disputed in the courts.

Some creditors are denied the opportunity to vote on the plan. Those creditors whose claims are not impaired under the plan proposal are deemed to have accepted the plan without a vote (11 U.S.C. §1129(a)(8)). If the treatment proposed under the plan "leaves unaltered the legal, equitable, and contractual rights to which such claim or interest entitles" the creditor, then the creditor's claim is deemed unimpaired (11 U.S.C. §1124(1)). Some collection rights can be lost and the claim is nonetheless deemed unimpaired for voting purposes (11 U.S.C. §1124(2)). The plan may propose to cure pre-plan defaults, to pay damages for those defaults, and to reinstate the maturity of the claims without legally impairing the creditor's interest (11 U.S.C. §1124(2)). Obviously, reinstatement of the original loan agreement denies the creditor its right to accelerate the loan and demand payment, but the Code treats reinstatement as leaving the creditor's interest unimpaired. In effect, this provision permits the DIP to cash out a recalcitrant creditor by paying that creditor its claim value and proceeding with the reorganization for the benefit of the remaining creditors. Only creditors whose rights are altered by the plan have the opportunity to vote with their class on whether the plan should or should not be confirmed. In effect, says the Code, only those with skin in the game will vote on the outcome.

The creditors' primary protection is in their voting rights, and it is not surprising that a great deal of informal negotiation goes on in putting together a plan proposal that will receive adequate votes for confirmation. At the same time, the Code sharply limits the powers of dissenting creditors. If they are unable to control their class, they lose most of their power in a reorganization. Except on very limited grounds, a minority of unsecured creditors cannot wreck a reorganization that the majority of creditors support.

In large cases, much of the negotiation goes on through the creditors' committee, which was discussed in greater detail in Chapter 2. The creditors' committee is composed of the seven largest unsecured creditors that are willing to serve (11 U.S.C. §1102(b)(1)). The committee will often take an active role in shaping the plan and in lobbying other creditors for or against its acceptance. Additional committees of unsecured creditors, secured creditors, or equity holders may be formed as well, particularly in a complex case (11 U.S.C. §1102(a)(2)). Acceptance of a Chapter 11 plan by the creditors' committee is often regarded as practically — although not officially — critical to the successful confirmation of the plan. The debtor's need to get the creditors' committee's votes — and to win the votes of other creditors — gives the committee strong leverage in many plan negotiations.

Prior to the new rules on small business debtors, creditors' committees were rarely formed in small business bankruptcies. No creditor had sufficient interest, and the estate might not generate assets to cover the expenses of the committee. As noted earlier, the new provisions that will give a small business debtor an exemption from application of all the extra restrictions otherwise imposed on it may increase incentives for such debtor businesses to rally their creditors to form a committee.

Other Creditor Protections

Although their power is limited, dissenting creditors enjoy a few basic protections granted to all creditors. These protections permit dissenting creditors to stop a reorganization that does not meet certain minimal standards — even if the majority of creditors are in favor of the plan.

The central protection offered each creditor individually is that, unless the creditor consents to lesser treatment, it must receive at least as much in the Chapter 11 reorganization as it would have received in a hypothetical Chapter 7 liquidation (11 U.S.C. §1129(a)(7)(A)(ii)). This provision is generally referred to as the "best interest test," that is, the plan cannot be confirmed if it is not in the best interest of each creditor. The calculation for the best interest test accounts for the time value of money, so that the creditor that would receive $100 at liquidation on the date of the confirmation hearing would be entitled to $100 plus interest if it had to wait for payment over time under the plan process. The best interest test illustrates a basic requirement of the Chapter 11 process: If Chapter 11 does not produce at least as much value as a Chapter 7 liquidation for each creditor, any dissenting creditor can prevent confirmation of the plan.

In addition, even if all parties consent to the Chapter 11 plan, the court must find that the plan is feasible (11 U.S.C. §1129(a)(11)). The court has an independent obligation to confirm a plan only if confirmation is not likely to be followed by liquidation or further proceedings in bankruptcy, unless such an alternative is specified in the plan (11 U.S.C. §1129(a)(11)). This means that the court exercises some supervisory control over the debtor business, refusing to confirm plans that are unlikely to succeed. In practice, the court is likely to have little reason to question the feasibility of a plan if all the parties consent to it, and the court's limited time and resources give little opportunity for an independent judgment. Nonetheless, this provision requires the plan proponent to offer evidence regarding feasibility in its initial proposal, and it permits any dissenting party to bring to the court the question of whether the business proposal in the plan makes any sense.

To maintain the distributional scheme of Chapter 11, some priority claimants must be repaid in full, unless they agree to lesser treatment. Administrative expense priorities receive the best treatment in Chapter 11. They must be paid in full on the date the plan goes into effect (11 U.S.C. §1129(a)(9)(A)). Other priority claimants may be paid over time, but repayment in full includes the time value of money, so these claimants receive interest to compensate them for the loss involved in being paid over time. The present value of employee priority wage claims, contributions to employee benefit plans, grain and fishing priorities, priority deposit claims, and the claims of interim creditors in involuntary bankruptcies may be repaid over the life of the plan (11 U.S.C. §1129(a)(9)(B)). Tax claims must be paid in full within five years (11 U.S.C. §1129(a)(9)(C)). Once again, Chapter 11 mimics Chapter 7: Claimants who would have been paid first in a liquidation will be paid in full in a Chapter 11 reorganization.

The plan must also meet a number of technical requirements of disclosure and conformity with other regulatory laws. The plan must disclose the identity and affiliation of the post-confirmation officers, directors, or affiliates, and parties can object to the appointment or continuation of such individuals (11 U.S.C. §1129(a)(5)(A)). The proponent must disclose whether any insider will be employed or retained by the reorganized business (11 U.S.C. §1129(a)(5)(B)). By specifically requiring such disclosure in addition to the general admonitions on the adequacy of information necessary to make an informed investment decision, the Code gives the creditors another opportunity to discover conflicts of interest among those proposing the plan. If there are creditor classes with impaired claims, at least one of these classes must accept the plan, demonstrating the support of creditors who are sharing some of the losses in bankruptcy (11 U.S.C. §1129(a)(10)).

Finally, the court is given another ground on which to reject a consensual plan: If the plan is not proposed in good faith, it cannot be confirmed (11 U.S.C. §1129(a)(3)). Once again, the court is given little guidance on the meaning of "good faith." A small minority of courts, for example, have used this provision to refuse confirmation of plans in single-asset real estate cases that may otherwise meet confirmation requirements. These courts reason that such single-asset cases, involving only the debtor and one creditor, are inappropriate candidates for the collective proceeding of bankruptcy and should be resolved under state law. Other courts have used the good-faith provision to terminate repeat filings. The bankruptcy system gives the courts wide powers to reject a plan, once again moving from a fairly detailed technical analysis of plan requirements to an equity-based concept of giving the courts wide discretion to do justice.

Creditors may be entirely passive throughout this process, and the Code will nonetheless protect their rights. The DIP lists the claims against the estate in its filing schedules. If a claim is not listed as contingent, disputed, or unliquidated, the listing will constitute a claim against the estate and all the rights listed will attach, even if the creditor never files a claim with the court (11 U.S.C. §1111(a)). If the creditor challenges the DIP's listing, the court will determine the amount and the security of the claim (11 U.S.C. §502(b)). This permits creditors to ride through a bankruptcy, spending no money on additional collection or monitoring efforts, and still collect a pro rata distribution. It also permits a creditor to become active at any point in the process when the issues under consideration hold a particular interest for it.

Creditors need not stick around for the entire Chapter 11 process. Just as they can sell their debts outside bankruptcy, they can do the same once the debtor has filed for bankruptcy. The holder of the claim succeeds to the rights of the original claim holder. By offering a market for distressed debt, claims traders may change the Chapter 11 negotiations. Indeed, investment funds — often called "vulture investors" — buy up Chapter 11 debt with an eye toward an eventual profit when the business liquidates and pays quickly, when the business reorganizes and pays over time, or when the vulture investor takes over ownership of the business by buying up a controlling share of the debt. Plan confirmation, like every other part of Chapter 11, creates an opportunity to deal.

Nonconsensual Plans

One or more groups of creditors may vote against the confirmation of a plan, but the Code sets forth conditions under which the plan may nonetheless be confirmed. The procedure by which a plan is confirmed over the objection of one or more classes is colorfully referred to as a "cramdown": the plan is crammed down the objecting class's throat. In a cramdown, all of the provisions already discussed must be met, except for the requirement of consent of all the classes. If one or more classes dissent, the plan can be confirmed if it meets the other requirements and it meets some additional cramdown requirements.

Absolute Priority

The "absolute priority rule" is designed to protect all creditors in a cramdown. Under the rule, a reorganization plan cannot provide for compensation for junior classes unless the senior classes either accept the plan or are compensated in full. In most plans, the secured creditors will have received the value of their collateral and the priority claimants will have been repaid in full. The next claimants, usually the unsecured creditors, can invoke the absolute priority rule, demanding repayment in full as a condition of any inferior class receiving any distribution from the estate (11 U.S.C. §1129(b)). In practice, this usually means the unsecured creditors want to be paid in full before the old stockholders can have the equity ownership of the new business. The provision applies to multiple classes, so that preferred stockholders, for example, retain rights in the Chapter 11 proceeding ahead of general stockholders (11 U.S.C. §1129(b)(2)(C)). This provision codifies the principle of corporate law that, when a business is dissolved, creditors are paid ahead of equity holders.[8]

If unsecured creditors as a class neither accept the plan nor receive payment in full, then the debtor-business's equity holders may not participate in the plan — that is, they may not retain their ownership of the business. Instead, ownership passes to the unsecured creditors, on a pro rata basis, or is sold to a third party, with the proceeds distributed to the unsecured creditors.

In a large business reorganization with publicly traded stock, this might mean that the dissenting class of unsecured creditors would be paid under the plan in part with cash distributions and in part with distributions of the stock of the newly emerging business. In the reorganization of a small business with an owner-manager, a new purchaser of the business might not emerge and the manager might not want to continue to work in the business without an equity interest. In effect, the absolute priority rule as applied to small cases may result in the forced liquidation of the business.

In fact, it is a third kind of case that presents the biggest dilemma when a business is trying to cram down a Chapter 11 plan: single asset real estate cases, or "SAREs." When Congress created Chapter 11 in 1978, it abolished Chapter XII, which was a separate reorganization chapter for real estate cases, but it could not abolish the economic factors that make such cases quite different from the typical Chapter 11. SAREs are defined in Section 101(51B) of the Code. A typical example would be a corporation or partnership whose only real asset is an apartment house or office building and whose only substantial debt is the mortgage on it. Such a case often amounts to a two-party struggle between the owner and the mortgage lender, with few other creditors or employees involved.

Such cases stirred a lot of controversy in the first two decades after the adoption of the Code,[9] particularly in the context of the absolute priority rule. The Supreme Court reviewed such a case in *Bank of America National Trust and Savings Assoc. v. 203 N. LaSalle St. Partnership.*[10] The court held that the real estate partnership could not simply buy the equity in the business as part of its plan confirmation without giving others an opportunity to bid. The case ducked larger questions concerning when old equity could refinance the business in return for retaining ownership, and further litigation will surely follow.

In the context of a small business in which there is no business without the current owner-operator, as a practical matter the creditors may accede to continued participation by old equity. Of course, not all equity owners have either the desire or the financial wherewithal to participate in financing a reorganization. Even if they do, application of the absolute priority rule, especially after *203 N. LaSalle*, can be a difficult barrier.

The 1111(b) Election

One more provision regarding plan confirmations can affect either consensual or cramdown plans. The undersecured creditor has special rights to elect how it will be treated under the plan. The device is called the "1111(b) election," named after the Code section that provides for it.

A secured creditor may agree by contract that it will look only to its collateral for satisfaction of its debt. Such a creditor is called "nonrecoursed." In bankruptcy, this means that it has an allowed secured claim to the value of the collateral, but no deficiency claim if it is undersecured. The 1111(b) election permits this nonrecourse creditor to convert its loan to recourse against the estate, so that it has a participating unsecured claim as well (11 U.S.C. §1111(b)(1)(A)). Congressional debates over this provision focused on whether a debtor business organized as a single-asset entity, such as an apartment building or office building, would take advantage of Chapter 11 to reorganize when real estate prices were depressed, promise to pay the liquidation value of the building over time in the Chapter 11 plan, and profit handsomely if the market rebounded after the plan confirmation. Because the Code gives the non-recourse creditor a right to recourse against the estate, the creditor also has voting rights in the plan confirmation, a right to absolute priority if it dissents and controls its unsecured class, and pro rata participation in plan distributions.

Other undersecured creditors can use the 1111(b) election to accomplish a different end. The undersecured creditor whose claim is bifurcated into its secured and unsecured portions for treatment under the plan is permitted to waive its unsecured claim and demand instead full repayment of its total claim (11 U.S.C. §1111(b)(1)(B)). The election does not permit the creditor to demand the present value of the claim, simply the actual number of dollars to be paid under the claim. The dollars may be paid over the entire life of the plan without giving the creditor any interest to compensate for the delay in repayment (11 U.S.C. §1129(b)(2)(A)(i)(II)).

An example may help illustrate: A secured creditor owed a debt of $1,000,000 and having a security interest in collateral valued at $600,000 can waive its unsecured claim for $400,000 and demand that the plan pay the full $1,000,000 on its claim. The plan must still provide for the present value of the allowed secured claim (which is the present value of the collateral, $600,000). This means that if the claim is to be paid off in one year, the plan must provide at least $662,830 to satisfy the allowed secured claim or, if it is to be paid off in ten years, the plan must provide for payments totaling $1,624,220 (based on a hypothetical present value calculated at 10 percent interest compounded annually). These payments meet the requirements of 11 U.S.C. §1129(b)(2)(A)(i)(II). If the debtor made the 1111(b) election, an additional requirement is imposed: In the one-year payout case, the plan would have to provide for $1,000,000 (the total claim), not just $662,830 (the allowed secured claim). But in the ten-year payout case, the 1111(b) election would impose no new requirements. Section 1111(b) would be satisfied because the plan provides for repayment of $1,624,220 (the allowed secured claim), which exceeds $1,000,000 (the total claim). As the example shows, the 1111(b) election yields something to the creditor only in certain factual cases. Its primary protection is to give a creditor the opportunity to resist a short "cash out" of the undersecured creditor's interest.

The 1111(b) election is rarely invoked, perhaps because of the inordinate difficulty of reading the provision. The election provides undersecured creditors with a strategic choice that has its greatest effect if the plan proposes a quick payout of secured debt. The threat to invoke an 1111(b) election can dramatically change the shape that a DIP's proposed plan takes, sometimes causing an adjustment from a short plan to a long plan to cope with the higher secured debt.

Discharge

The debts of corporations and partnerships are not discharged in Chapter 7 (11 U.S.C. §727(a)(1)). But businesses that can successfully confirm a reorganization plan in Chapter 11 do receive a discharge of all debt that arose before the confirmation (11 U.S.C. §1141(d)(1)). For those businesses that confirm a Chapter 11 plan that liquidates the business, however, the discharge remains unavailable (11 U.S.C. §1141(d)(3)). Individual debtors using Chapter 11 follow the discharge rules laid out for them elsewhere in the Code (11 U.S.C. §1141(d)(2)).

The scope of the corporate debtor's discharge is broad. When the Chapter 11 plan is confirmed, the claims of creditors, equity security holders, and partners are discharged, and the emerging company is vested with the property of the estate "free and clear of all claims and interests" on those claims (11 U.S.C. §1141(a), (c)). Claims are discharged regardless of how the claimant voted on the plan or whether the creditor even filed a proof of claim (11 U.S.C. §1141(d)(1)(A)).

The Code is clear that discharge is only for the Chapter 11 business. Guarantors, partners, sureties, insurers, co-debtors, and others who may be liable on the discharged debt may seek a discharge, but they must file their own bankruptcies to accomplish that end (11 U.S.C. §524(e)). Some courts have used their equitable powers under 11 U.S.C. §105(a) to enjoin permanently any collection against a named party, such as a partner or a guarantor, which has the same effect as a discharge of the co-debtor, if such a move withstands appellate review.[11] Courts typically refuse to extend the automatic stay for such permanent injunctions unless they believe it is essential to do so in order to confirm a successful reorganization. The court will generally demand that the party profiting from such a move put as much into the reorganization as it would have if it had filed its own bankruptcy. Even in such circumstances, there is considerable controversy over the appropriateness of permitting such a non-debtor party to enjoy a permanent injunction from debt collection.

Discharge is granted at confirmation in a Chapter 11 proceeding, rather than being withheld until the debtor completes the payments proposed under the plan (11 U.S.C. §1141(d)). The Code mandates that the debtor and any successor carry out the plan, presumably making the debtor liable under non-bankruptcy law for breach of any obligation promised under the plan (11 U.S.C. §1142(a)). The court may order the debtor or any other party to do what is necessary to consummate the plan, such as issue securities or relinquish control of property (11 U.S.C. §1142(b)).

The court may revoke an order of confirmation. If the confirmation was secured by fraud, the court may issue new orders revoking the plan and the discharge and protecting any parties who relied on the plan in good faith (11 U.S.C. §1144). The statute of limitations for this action is brief, however, extending only 180 days after the confirmation order has been entered.

No-Discharge Plans

While most Chapter 11 plans are focused on the survival of a viable business, some are not. Chapter 11 may be used for liquidation of the business (11 U.S.C. §1123(b)(4)). Why would any business liquidate in Chapter 11 rather than in Chapter 7 or outside bankruptcy? Chapter 11 may offer a more orderly liquidation that will maximize returns to the creditors. In addition, Chapter 11, unlike non-bankruptcy proceedings and the somewhat more confined rules of Chapter 7, leaves open more options for settlement of disputes and distribution of the assets to the creditors. Moreover, because a Chapter 11 case can be liquidated without a trustee, avoiding the expense of trustee's fees that would reduce an already meager return to creditors may seem attractive.

Liquidating plans reveal the enormous flexibility of Chapter 11. The business (or the appointed trustee, if that is what the parties prefer) is given a wide range of options to sell assets of the business. Sometimes the liquidating plan provides for the mechanism by which assets will be sold over time. A typical example would be the conveyance of some or all of the estate's assets to a liquidating trust managed by a trustee appointed through the plan.

The line between a reorganization and a liquidation is not always clear. Most businesses emerge from Chapter 11 slimmer than they were when they entered. The ability to shed property during the course of the bankruptcy under Section 363(b) sales (with court approval, of course) may put a business on a track to liquidation — or may shrink it enough to let it succeed. Alternatively, some parts of the business may be sold off in chunks large enough to constitute viable businesses on their own. Flexibility often means that the outcomes scatter along a continuum of reorganization to liquidation.

One of the largest bankruptcies in history was the implosion of the Enron Corporation. Although the proceedings were conducted entirely in Chapter 11, the business was liquidated, eventually paying out about 20 cents on the dollar. In such a case, the Chapter 11 plan is largely about how to allocate the post-sale assets among the warring parties. No one was looking toward the revival of company.

The Role of Valuation

Although the technical rules for confirmation of a plan are fairly straightforward (with some notable exceptions), a great deal of flexibility necessarily inheres in the Code structure. Virtually every Code requirement depends on valuation of the going-concern business or valuation of its individual assets. The legal rules for the treatment of undersecured and over-secured debt, for example, are unambiguous. For example, a creditor with an outstanding loan of $100,000 and a security interest in a machine now valued at $60,000 will participate as an unsecured creditor for $40,000 and will receive the present value of its $60,000 secured claim as part of a confirmed plan. But if the machine is valued at $120,000, the plan must offer the same creditor the present value of the full $100,000 loan amount plus interim interest on the loan, calculated from the time of filing until confirmation, and the creditor has no vote in plan confirmation.

Much of the flexibility in the plan process comes from the fact that the exact value of the machine or of the going-concern business or of any other property, interest, or obligation is unknown. Valuation is subject to estimation, to conjecture, to guess—to everything but a real sale. Except when the plan proponent deliberately uses liquidation to reshape the business and to generate cash, the assets stay in the business and are "valued." As a result, the statutory guarantees and the resulting negotiating positions are necessarily based on uncertain projections of value. A creditor's rights are not nearly so certain as the Code would suggest, nor can it be completely clear when the plan proponent has met the Code's obligations.

To compound the difficulties of valuation, the value of a going-concern business may fluctuate. The business may recover simply because the market has gotten better or because business operations have improved. The DIP may enhance the value of the estate by exercising the Code-granted powers to reshape the business. The plan negotiation process may go well and thus convince more people that the business will survive. All these possibilities affect the value of the going-concern business, the price for which it could be sold, and the amount it can reasonably promise to repay after confirmation. As the parties negotiate around these uncertainties, tentative plans may emerge, re-form, and emerge again.

The concept that underlies the consensual plan is that the parties in Chapter 11 are granted certain rights that they may demand in court and that those rights, in turn, will shape the leverage the parties will exercise in plan negotiations. But most of those rights are based on uncertain and shifting valuations. In a world of uncertainty, the Bankruptcy Code puts a premium on reshaping the bankrupt business through negotiation and consent.

Legal rights are rarely disputed in consensual plans, but the payouts that the parties finally settle on clearly reflect their rights. The settlements reflect a number of economic and business realities as well. The secured creditor with some rights who is also willing to serve as a post-petition financer, and the trade creditor who has some collection rights as an unsecured creditor but who is also essential to the long-term survival of the business both exercise a combination of economic and statutory powers.

MOVING FASTER WITH A PRE-PACKAGED PLAN

A Chapter 11 often comes as a stunning surprise to the creditors and employees of a business. But for those on the inside, the business problems may have been evident for quite a while. It is not uncommon for a business in trouble to reach out to the bankruptcy lawyers long before any public recognition of the problems has occurred. If the lawyers and the business can line up a deal in advance of a Chapter 11 filing, they may opt for a fast-track Chapter 11. Keeping with the fast-food parlance of ready-to-go eating, such a plan is known as a pre-pack.

A pre-pack lives in the netherworld between consent and force. In order to get a pre-pack going, the business needs the cooperation and eventual consent of many of its creditors. But if the business had the consent of *all* the creditors, there would be no need for any bankruptcy at all. The parties would simply do a voluntary workout. A pre-packaged bankruptcy is one in which a deal has been struck with the financers and some of the creditors, but the hammer of bankruptcy is needed to make certain that everyone comes along.

The basic idea behind a pre-pack is that much of the bargaining that takes place inside a Chapter 11 is conducted before the filing. During the pre-bankruptcy period the business arranges for post-petition financing, identifies the contracts it intends to assume or reject, and negotiates with creditors over how much debt forgiveness will be necessary for the business to survive. Most critically, the business must work out a real business plan for its post-reorganization recovery so that it has a credible story to take to the lenders. In fact, a business that is trying to hammer out a pre-pack will go so far as to draft its plan and try to sell it to some or all of the creditors, engaging in pre-petition disclosure and solicitation of votes for the impending Chapter 11.

Because the actions taken pre-bankruptcy are designed to fulfill the bankruptcy requirements involving solicitation and disclosure, the bankruptcy court will eventually review the pre-bankruptcy activities to determine their legal sufficiency. Section 1126(b) holds that pre-petition voting will be ratified in bankruptcy so long as the pre-petition solicitation complied with all applicable disclosure laws and regulations. If the company's solicitations comply with the non-bankruptcy laws, such as any applicable SEC rules, and with the bankruptcy solicitation rules of Section 1125(a), the votes will bind the creditors and can be used to confirm a plan. To make matters easier, under local rules adopted in some of the federal court districts around the country, including those in Delaware and Southern New York, pre-packs can proceed with far less public disclosure of information in bankruptcy court than the ordinary Chapter 11.

The business may begin solicitations pre-bankruptcy and complete them after the bankruptcy has been filed, but a post-filing solicitation will mean that the judge must approve the disclosure statement. That is likely to slow down the process. In a true pre-pack the business has all its ducks in a row before the bankruptcy petition is filed.

For those accustomed to the crawl of legal proceedings, the speed of a pre-packaged plan can be breathtaking. Courts have proudly declared that they have managed pre-packs in thirty days or less. The speed is particularly important to a business that does not want headlines about its financial troubles. Emphasizing an already-negotiated deal to emerge from bankruptcy can take some of the sting out of a bankruptcy announcement. That is precisely what a pre-pack permits.

While the advocates of pre-packs point to their speed and low costs, not everyone finds them attractive. Creditors that were not a party to the initial negotiations or, worse, that opposed the business's plans, have a hard time fighting the onrush of the pre-packaged plan. The creditors are lined up, financing is in place, the orders get signed quickly, and the whole reorganization — including the discharge of substantial amounts of debt and payments to favored lenders — is over before it begins. For those who think the scrutiny of the courts and the detailed process involve important safeguards, the speed is viewed with great suspicion. For those who think lower costs and less paperwork are the beginning of a deal made in Heaven, pre-packs look like a brilliant business innovation.

POLICY CONSIDERATIONS

Nowhere is the collective nature of the Chapter 11 proceeding clearer than in plan confirmation. Each party works to ensure that its own individual interests are protected, but the Code enforces a kind of cooperation designed to enhance the collective interests of the creditors and to give the business the best opportunity to survive. The Code reduces the holdout power of each creditor by restricting voting to classes and by permitting majorities to silence dissenting minorities within classes. Secured creditors have some power to demand repayment in Chapter 11, but their powers are sharply limited for the collective good. They can be forced to participate in a Chapter 11 proceeding, taking payments over time and thereby involuntarily extending credit to the post-reorganization business. Unsecured creditors have even less individual power.

They may see part or even all of their outstanding debts discharged, and they may wait for payments for years.

The best-interest test imposed by the Code is an example of a technical requirement for confirmation that demonstrates the pervasiveness of a value-enhancement norm. The creditors in a Chapter 11 confirmation must do at least as well as they would have done in a Chapter 7 confirmation. If, for example, the liquidation of the estate would have brought a pro rata distribution of 15 cents for each dollar of unsecured debt, a plan proposing a 20 percent repayment to the unsecured creditors is confirmable. But if the liquidation would have yielded 30 cents for each dollar of unsecured debt, a single objecting creditor can halt the confirmation of the plan. If a Chapter 11 plan will reduce the payout to creditors, then it cannot be confirmed without the consent of those injured. The best-interest test reinforces the goal of using reorganization to enhance value, not to diminish it.

The best-interest test also demonstrates the distributive values provided in Chapter 11. While the test establishes a baseline promise to the creditors, it does not require that only the creditors capture all the benefits of a reorganization. If the creditors get at least as much as they would have gotten in a liquidation, the Code requirement is satisfied. This leaves open the possibility that additional assets generated by the reorganizing business may be retained by the business to enhance its stability and long-term survival prospects. This suggests that successful reorganization — with its consequent effects on employees, taxing authorities, suppliers, and a host of other entities — is itself a permissible goal. The value-enhancing benefits of Chapter 11 are not restricted to creditor repayments.

At the same time, the statutory rights granted to creditors who have little extraneous leverage illustrates the distributional objectives of the Code. For example, the right of tort victims to share pro rata in distributions with other unsecured creditors in their class or the right of a secured creditor to get at least the present value of its collateral are minimal guarantees that prevent the creditors with more leverage from taking everything. These statutory guarantees make certain that creditors collectively profit from the reorganization, as opposed to having just a handful of creditors capture all the value.

The cramdown plan fits a similar pattern. It incorporates all the requirements of the consensual plan — and all its normative values — except the plan can be confirmed even if some classes vote against it. By permitting confirmation without the consent of all classes, the Code necessarily realigns the power of participants in the bankruptcy process. Cramdowns diminish the power of creditors, particularly their power to hold out for better treatment than the minimum amounts guaranteed elsewhere in the Code. The availability of the cramdown option also increases the number of bankrupt businesses that are reorganized rather than liquidated, demonstrating once again a preference in the Code for reorganization.

The absolute priority rule restricts the DIP's use of the cramdown by requiring that equity holders retain no ownership in the reorganizing business unless superior classes either have accepted the plan or have received payment in full. This fine-tunes the balance of power among the parties. If the DIP wants to confirm a plan that includes retaining equity ownership, it will either have to pay the creditors in full or negotiate for their cooperation. If, however, the DIP wants to sell the business and distribute the assets to the creditors, a dissenting class cannot block that action unless some other Code requirement has been violated. Thus, the power of creditors if they choose to dissent is restricted; they can block some actions but not others. The balance achieved is one that is designed to enhance reorganization, but to provide some creditor protection as well.

The Bankruptcy Code establishes a rough allocation of power among the parties in interest in a bankruptcy case, and the courts refine that allocation with their interpretation of the statutory provisions. Whenever a court redefines the requirements of a Chapter 11 plan, it necessarily redistributes power among the parties. Some Code provisions are interpreted on a case-by-case basis, such as plan feasibility. Other provisions require uniform interpretations notwithstanding the ambiguity of the Code language, such as the question of the DIP's power to classify its creditors to enhance adoption of the plan. The courts refine the balance that affects the terms on which plans are confirmed and determine whether some plans are confirmed at all.

Finally, it is worth noting that the issues that arise in plan confirmation highlight particularly the policy to keep the bankruptcy system voluntary. Although the bankruptcy goals of enhancing the value of the estate and making deliberate distributional decisions are evident throughout virtually every aspect of the Code, it is easy to overlook the impact of these provisions on whether bankruptcy is made sufficiently attractive that debtors will choose to use it when their businesses are faltering. Every aspect of plan confirmation that deals with those who make the decision to file — management in large businesses and owner-managers in small businesses — has an effect on whether debtors will find Chapter 11 a plausible alternative to a non-bankruptcy workout under state law or a disorganized collapse of the business.

One of the principal objections to the old Chapter X was that it always ousted management from power. The drafters of the 1978 Code knew that if they continued in that direction, few managers would choose bankruptcy even when the business and the creditors could profit from such a move. The same concerns are implicated in the plan-confirmation rules. If management fears an immediate loss of control over running the business because it cannot count on a reasonable period of exclusivity within which to propose a plan, it is likely to be more reluctant to file. If an owner-manager of a small business faces automatic loss of its business in a Chapter 11, it will feel an even more acute reluctance to file.

In addition, plan-confirmation provisions, with their necessary impact on how management and owners see the progress of the Chapter 11 proceeding and on their participation in an eventual reorganization, also implicate another careful bankruptcy balance: the balance between the interests of the decision makers who file for bankruptcy and the interests of other parties in the case. Although the Code sharply restricts the power of management and owners during the bankruptcy proceedings and in plan reorganizations, it offers them sufficient protection so that most who enter bankruptcy fully expect to make a number of concessions to their creditors but also to maintain control over the business. If this careful balance were upset, bankruptcy policy goals would be compromised.

CONCLUSION

The bankruptcy system provides a forum for parties to decide together who must share the losses of a business failure. These parties will be forced to yield some collection rights for the collective benefit of the creditors and to implement the distributional norms of the Code. The Chapter 11 plan provisions set the technical rules for plan confirmation and allocate negotiating power to the creditors, but the parties generally negotiate their own conclusion to the business. They may ultimately negotiate a consensual plan that the court confirms, a liquidation of the business, or a dismissal of the bankruptcy case and a return to general collection law. In bankruptcy, perhaps more than any other area of commercial law, the parties bargain for a new future in the shadow of the legal rules that can be enforced in court.

~ 6 ~

Jurisdiction,
Procedure, and
Transnational Cases

A BROAD GRANT OF JURISDICTION

Chapter 11 works because it is powerful. As a business begins to fail, the instinct runs deep for everyone that is owed money to grab it and run. Only a very powerful law can manage a collective resolution of an otherwise-chaotic business failure. And only force can wrest preferential payments out of the hands those who know that once they let go, they are unlikely to see that money ever again. To reach the goals of enhancing the value of the estate and efficiently distributing that value to the creditors of the estate, the bankruptcy laws need to be grounded in the broadest possible jurisdictional reach.

Notwithstanding the constitutional grant of power to Congress to establish "uniform Laws on the subject of Bankruptcies throughout the United States,"[1] bankruptcy laws did not always enjoy a broad jurisdictional reach. The old 1898 Bankruptcy Act was built on a complex jurisdictional labyrinth. Prior to 1978, Congress gave the bankruptcy courts only a sliver of jurisdiction to resolve the problems facing the failing business.

Under the old Bankruptcy Act, most disputes related to the bankruptcy were resolved in state courts. The system was extraordinarily confusing, particularly for the non-bankruptcy specialist. It was also expensive, burning up time and money that could have better been spent trying to save the business. The jurisdictional and procedural snares of the 1898 Act were widely perceived as obstacles to the efficient liquidation and reorganization of bankrupt businesses. To make the system more efficient, the Bankruptcy Code of 1978 was designed to make the bankruptcy courts much more powerful.

The Code Solution — and Problem

By 1978, both the House and the Senate agreed on a solution to the jurisdictional and procedural problems of the bankruptcy system: expand bankruptcy jurisdiction to include all disputes related to the bankruptcy proceeding. Any disputes affecting the estate would be swept into the bankruptcy courts for timely resolution. There would be no more litigation over jurisdiction and delays for other proceedings, and cases could proceed expeditiously.

But the House and the Senate differed over the structure of the bankruptcy courts. They agreed on the central principle that the bankruptcy courts should be run by judges who functioned only as judicial officers, not as case administrators. They differed sharply, however, about the constitutional status of these judges. The House proposed the creation of separate bankruptcy courts in which the bankruptcy judges would be appointed for life by the president under Article III of the Constitution, using a process much like the one used in the appointment of district court judges. The Senate, however, proposed to leave the bankruptcy judges in an inferior role as assistants to the district judge, serving for an appointed term.

The 1978 Bankruptcy Code reflects a compromise of these views. Bankruptcy courts were created with broad jurisdictional authority to hear controversies and to issue orders that would affect bankruptcy estates. The bankruptcy judges were empowered to exercise virtually all bankruptcy jurisdiction. But bankruptcy courts were denominated as "adjuncts" to the district court, not independent federal courts — a distinction that seemed to have little substantive consequence at the time. The Code provided that bankruptcy judges would be appointed by the president, but they would not have life tenure.

In 1982, the Supreme Court ruled that the compromise in the 1978 Code was unconstitutional. In *Northern Pipeline Construction v. Marathon Pipe Line*,[2] Justice Brennan, writing for a plurality of four justices, held that the creation of non–Article III courts to handle cases within a broad jurisdictional range in the bankruptcy system was constitutionally impermissible. The adjunct relationship between the district courts and the bankruptcy courts was insufficient to overcome this defect. The Court recognized that certain aspects of the jurisdiction might permissibly be given to the bankruptcy courts, but it ruled that the entire system was unconstitutional because it vested the "judicial power" under Article III of the Constitution in judges who did not have life tenure as Article III requires. Justice Rehnquist, joined by Justice O'Connor, concurred on the narrower ground that the dispute presented in the *Marathon* case was a traditional common-law contract suit brought by a DIP against a party unrelated to the bankruptcy case and was therefore beyond the constitutional scope of the bankruptcy court's jurisdiction. Dissenting Justices White and Powell and Chief Justice Burger would have upheld the constitutionality of the 1978 Code. Chief Justice Burger also wrote a separate dissent in which he outlined how the constitutional defects identified by the majority could be corrected — an analysis sharply disputed by Justice Brennan.

The issue was put clearly to Congress: Either make the bankruptcy judges Article III judges with lifetime appointments or reduce the scope of their jurisdiction, forcing the Article III district courts to increase their workloads to include more bankruptcy disputes. But Congress refused to act.

The Supreme Court twice stayed application of its *Marathon* holding to give Congress time to recast bankruptcy jurisdiction, but Congress still did not act. In the meantime, the Judicial Conference of the United States, acting through the Administrative Office of the U.S. Courts, developed a model "Emergency Rule" to be used if Congress did not amend the defective Bankruptcy Code before the Supreme Court's stay expired. On Christmas Eve, 1982, *Marathon* went into effect. The Emergency Rule was promptly adopted by the district court judges of each district to govern referral of matters to bankruptcy judges. The rule remained in effect until Congress amended the jurisdictional scheme in 1984.

Under the Emergency Rule, bankruptcy judges could hear and make final orders in all "core proceedings," a phrase adopted from Justice Brennan's observation that "the restructuring of debtor-creditor relations . . . is at the core of the federal bankruptcy power."[3] In "related proceedings," bankruptcy judges could hear matters and recommend findings, conclusions, and proposed orders to the district court, which could then make a de novo review and enter a final order. The constitutionality of the Emergency Rule was upheld by the courts of appeals that considered it, but the scheme was never reviewed by the Supreme Court. A few constitutional law scholars doubted whether the rule addressed the constitutional defects cited in the *Marathon* opinion.

A Constitutional Knot

After *Marathon*, Congress faced the same split in trying to cure the constitutional infirmities that it had faced when the Code was originally drafted. The House wanted to create Article III bankruptcy judges, while the Senate wanted the judges to remain adjuncts to the district court judges. A number of substantive amendments to the Code were also proposed, including those to restrict consumer debtors' rights in bankruptcy and to alter the treatment of collective bargaining agreements in Chapter 11.

Compromises were achieved only in the final hours before the bill passed, with the result that there is little useful legislative history and the language of the amendments is not a model of clarity. The Senate approach prevailed once again. Under the 1984 amendments, bankruptcy judges would not become Article III judges. Instead, they "constitute a unit of the district court to be known as the bankruptcy court for that district" (28 U.S.C. §151).

The bankruptcy judges "serve as judicial officers of the United States district court" (28 U.S.C. §152(a)(1)). They are appointed by the Courts of Appeals for their respective circuits for fourteen-year terms (28 U.S.C. §152(a)(2)). After fourteen years on the bench, a judge can be renewed or a new judge can be appointed in her place. During the term, judges are subject to removal "only for incompetence, misconduct, neglect of duty, or physical or mental disability and only by the judicial council of the circuit" (28 U.S.C. §152(e)).

In an attempt to correct the constitutional defects of the 1978 Code, the 1984 amendments curtail the jurisdiction of the bankruptcy courts. The statute places bankruptcy jurisdiction in the district court, then permits the district court to refer cases to the bankruptcy court. All "original and exclusive jurisdiction of all cases under [the Bankruptcy Code]" is vested in the district court (28 U.S.C. §1334(a)). The district court also has exclusive jurisdiction over all property of the business as of the commencement of the case and over all property of the estate, regardless of where such property is located (28 U.S.C. §1334(e)). In addition, the district court has "original but not exclusive jurisdiction of all civil proceedings arising under title 11, or arising in or related to cases under title 11" (28 U.S.C. §1334(b)). The term "civil proceedings" is chosen to give the broadest possible sweep. The legislative history of the provision encompasses both action during the pending case and resolution of issues that arise after the case is closed. This means, for example, that actions to determine the validity of securities issued under a reorganization plan might remain within the bankruptcy jurisdiction of the district court. Not surprisingly, the district court's "original but not exclusive" jurisdiction has complicated the bankruptcy scheme.

Despite this broad grant of jurisdiction to the district courts, they do not hear all proceedings in bankruptcy cases. Further complicating the jurisdictional scheme are provisions that make jurisdiction in the district court rest on the types of proceedings to be heard. There is no provision for a district court to abstain in a bankruptcy case, which means that the district court may not, for example, refuse to take bankruptcy filings (28 U.S.C. §1334). But if a proceeding "arises under" or "arises in" a case once it has been filed, a district court may abstain "in the interest of justice, or in the interest of comity with State courts or respect for State law" (28 U.S.C. §1334(a), (c)(I)). In addition, a district court must abstain in a proceeding based on a state-law claim or cause of action "related to," but not arising under or arising in, a bankruptcy case, if the state-law claim has commenced and can be timely resolved in a state-law forum (28 U.S.C. §1334(c)(2)). There is, of course, an exception to mandatory abstention if there are independent grounds (such as diversity) for federal jurisdiction. Finally, the district court's decision to abstain is not reviewable (28 U.S.C. §1334(d)).

Whether the district court has exclusive jurisdiction, permissive jurisdiction, or no jurisdiction depends on whether the proceeding "arises under" or "arises in" a case or instead is "related to" a case. Unfortunately, precise definitions of the key terms are lacking. The terms first appeared in the broad grant of jurisdiction in the 1978 Bankruptcy Code, but before *Marathon* there was little reason to differentiate among the categories because the bankruptcy courts exercised jurisdiction in all cases. There are now reasons for differentiation, but the distinctions remain elusive.

Even when the district court has exclusive jurisdiction, the 1984 amendments do not contemplate that the court will actually hear every issue in every case. For actions that are "core proceedings," the district court may refer the case to the bankruptcy judge for hearing and determination (28 U.S.C. §157(a), (b)). In fact, every district court in the country has adopted a policy of automatic referral, although occasionally a district court will withdraw the referral in a particularly difficult case or a case of unusually widespread implications. Back in the 1980s, in the original Dalkon Shield implant cases involving then-giant A.H. Robins, for example, the district judge and the bankruptcy judge sat side by side on the bench and listened to arguments and disposed of motions together. That case was, however, a very rare exception.

Just as the district court may refer a case to the bankruptcy court, the district court also retains the power to "withdraw, in whole or in part, any case or proceeding" so referred (28 U.S.C. §157(d)). The court may withdraw its referral to the bankruptcy court on its own motion or on the motion of any party, and it may do so at any point in the proceeding (28 U.S.C. §157(d)). The 1984 amendments require the district court to withdraw proceedings that require "consideration of both title 11 and other laws of the United States regulating organizations or activities affecting interstate commerce" (28 U.S.C. §157(d)). Notwithstanding this seemingly broad requirement to withdraw proceedings from the bankruptcy courts, such withdrawals are rare in practice, particularly in many Chapter 11 cases.

The bankruptcy court sits as the trial court, issuing final orders that can be appealed to the district court (28 U.S.C. §§157(b)(1), 158(a)). For actions that are not core proceedings but "are otherwise related to a case under title 11," the district court may refer the case to the bankruptcy judge for proposed findings of fact and conclusions of law if the district court has jurisdiction (note the limitation imposed by mandatory abstention) (28 U.S.C. §157(c)). Appeals from the bankruptcy court's proposed orders are reviewed de novo, and final orders issue from the district court (28 U.S.C. §157(c)). The parties may consent to jurisdiction in the bankruptcy courts over a non-core proceeding, in which case review will be in the district court as if the matter were a core proceeding (28 U.S.C. §157(c)(2)). The 2005 amendments added a provision that slightly bolsters the status of the bankruptcy courts by permitting direct appeals from bankruptcy court to the Court of Appeals in limited circumstances (28 U.S.C. §158(d)).

Bankruptcy courts routinely hear both core matters and non-core matters related to a case. The distinction between the two is important for determining when the district court reviews final orders of the bankruptcy court on a clearly erroneous standard and when it only considers the bankruptcy court's proposed findings of fact and law and makes its own findings. The distinction between the types of cases and between the appropriate scope of review turns on whether the proceedings are "core proceedings" or "non-core proceedings." A bankruptcy judge determines whether a proceeding is a core proceeding (28 U.S.C. §157(b)(3)).

Once again, the definitions of the critical categories are somewhat elusive. The 1984 amendments list examples of core proceedings. They include matters concerning administration of the estate, allowance of claims, counterclaims against creditors of the estate, orders for obtaining credit, turnover of property of the estate, preference avoidance, violations of the automatic stay, recovery of fraudulent conveyances, testing the validity of liens, objections to discharge, confirmation of plans, and similar matters (28 U.S.C. §157(b)(2)). But the list is only suggestive, not exhaustive. The Code leaves open the possibility that other matters may be core proceedings, thus blurring the distinction between core and non-core proceedings.

Plenary jurisdiction had not seemed so foreign to most creditors who had had some experience with bankruptcy courts, but in the early 1980s, personal injury lawyers were suddenly hauled into bankruptcy court when their corporate defendants filed for bankruptcy protection. Trials stopped and negotiations took on a very different flavor. The PI lawyers were unhappy, very unhappy — and they deeply distrusted these bankruptcy judges who seemed to see their clients as just one more creditor group. As part of the jurisdictional reorganization of bankruptcy in 1984, personal injury and wrongful death claims against the estate receive special treatment. Those suits are not within the core jurisdiction of the bankruptcy judge under the reference from the district court, nor are they subject to the mandatory abstention accorded other state-law claims (28 U.S.C. §§157(b)(4),1334(c)(2)). Instead, these claims are tried by the federal district court, unless the parties consent to the jurisdiction of the bankruptcy court or unless the district court exercises its discretionary abstention to permit a state court to try the case (28 U.S.C. §§157(c)(2), 1334(c)(1)).

The jurisdictional structure is complex, but the grant of power to the district courts — and, in turn, to the bankruptcy courts — remains broad. Much of the language granting jurisdiction to the district courts is the same as that used in the 1978 Code. Even when jurisdiction is nonexclusive, it is generally greater than the jurisdiction of any competing court. For example, litigation in other courts is stayed automatically when a petition is filed, even though the district court may be called on later to make a decision to abstain or to remand the case (11 U.S.C. §§362, 105; 28 U.S.C. §§1334(c)(2), 1452(b)).

Despite the passage of time, the 1984 provisions dividing jurisdiction on the basis of whether proceedings are core or arising under, arising in, or related to the bankruptcy case have not yet been fully tested in the Supreme Court to determine whether they cure the constitutional infirmities identified in *Marathon*. Instead, the Circuit courts have ratified the constitutionality of the system generally. With few litigants raising the issue and no split in the circuits, the Supreme Court has had little reason to turn to this thorny constitutional question.

Appeals from the Bankruptcy Court

Appeals from the bankruptcy court have become an increasingly important part of the federal judicial workload.

The process by which bankruptcy cases find their way to the district courts and courts of appeals is complex. As noted earlier, the district court reviews the proposed findings of fact and conclusions of law regarding non-core matters referred to the bankruptcy court. As a jurisdictional matter, the district court makes a de novo review of any matters "to which any party has timely and specifically objected" and then enters final orders (28 U.S.C. §157(c)(1)). In effect, the district court is acting as the court of original, not appellate, jurisdiction.

In core matters referred to the bankruptcy court and in matters heard by consent of the parties, the district court operates as an appellate court. It hears appeals from final judgments, orders, and decrees of the bankruptcy court, and reviews them on a clearly erroneous basis. The district court may also grant motions to hear appeals from interlocutory orders and decrees from the bankruptcy court (28 U.S.C. §158(a)).

Since the district court's responsibility to hear appeals is mandatory rather than permissive if the matter at issue is a final order rather than an interlocutory order, the distinction between final and interlocutory orders becomes crucial to the appellate process. The general concept of finality embodied in other appellate litigation applies in the bankruptcy system as well, but bankruptcy cases present special problems. Bankruptcy cases often consist of one large case in which a number of proceedings must be resolved. Waiting to resolve one dispute until all are resolved would involve extraordinary delay and, potentially, a great waste of both the litigants' and the courts' resources.

Unlike a single lawsuit, a bankruptcy involves the reorganization of an entire business and may drag in thousands of parties — and thousands of disputes. To deal with these disputes effectively, the concept of finality in bankruptcy generally does not require that the entire case be resolved. Instead, parties may appeal a series of more limited questions. So, for example, a bankruptcy case might involve a dispute over whether a business could be adjudicated an involuntary bankrupt or whether a creditor received a voidable preference that it is now obligated to disgorge. Finality is resolved by applying generally applicable principles to these smaller questions. Not surprisingly, a conflicting body of case law has grown up regarding the question of finality in bankruptcy cases. Nonetheless, the process of treating some decisions as final before the whole case is resolved facilitates quicker final resolution of cases. Perhaps more important, it also permits key elements of a pending case (such as the resolution of a claim against the estate or the estate's recovery against another party) to be resolved so that the other elements of a workable plan can be negotiated without difficult contingency planning.

The Code provides an alternative route for appeal of a bankruptcy court order. The judicial council of a circuit may establish a bankruptcy appellate panel (BAP) composed of a group of bankruptcy judges from districts within the circuit, and the district judges may by majority vote authorize referral of appeals to these panel judges (28 U.S.C. §158(b)(1)). If the parties then consent in a particular case, the BAP exercises appellate jurisdiction, rather than the district court (28 U.S.C. §158(b)(1)).

After a district court or a BAP has issued a final order, judgment, or decree, an appeal may be taken to the court of appeals (28 U.S.C. §158(d)). There is no grant of jurisdiction for appeals from interlocutory orders. If the district court exercised original jurisdiction in a case, the court of appeals is the first appellate court. On an appeal from a BAP or from an appellate district court order, the court of appeals is the second level of appellate jurisdiction.

The Supreme Court exercises jurisdiction in bankruptcy cases in the same manner as it exercises jurisdiction in ordinary civil actions involving interpretation of federal statutes. It generally reviews judgments of the court of appeals by writ of certiorari, but the jurisdictional grounds for review by appeal also apply (28 U.S.C. §1254(1)).

CASE MANAGEMENT

Jury Trials

Does a party subject to the jurisdiction of the district court and, by referral, to that of the bankruptcy court, have a right to a jury trial in a bankruptcy proceeding? If so, will it be heard by the district court judge or by the bankruptcy judge?

Bankruptcy laws "do not affect any right to trial by jury that an individual had under applicable non-bankruptcy law with regard to a personal injury or wrongful death tort claim" (28 U.S.C. §1411). Because those cases are heard in the district court, the provision suggests that the district court may conduct jury trials in such cases (28 U.S.C. §157(b)(5)).

The U.S. Constitution governs the right to jury trials, providing that "[i]n suits at common law, where the value in controversy shall exceed twenty dollars, the right of trial by jury shall be preserved."[4] The right to jury trial guaranteed by the Constitution usually has been restricted to suits at common law, as opposed to actions in equity or those seeking equitable remedies. Bankruptcy law is generally equitable in nature, which has caused some commentators to conclude that there is no guaranteed right to a trial by jury in bankruptcy matters.

Congress authorized jury trials in bankruptcy court, but only if (a) the matter is otherwise within the bankruptcy court's jurisdiction, (b) the district court expressly authorizes it, and (c) the court has the consent of all parties (28 U.S.C. §157(e)). Otherwise, Congress has been pragmatic. Seeing no pressing problems on the horizon, Congress has shied away from any general jurisdictional issues. Bankruptcy judges, returning the favor, have shied away from jury trials, keeping their number very low.

Contempt Powers

The clearest statement delineating the bankruptcy courts' use of contempt powers is found in the Bankruptcy Rules. They provide that the bankruptcy judge may summarily issue an order of contempt for actions committed in the presence of the court and also may issue an order, after notice and a hearing, for other contempt actions (Bankruptcy Rule 9020(a), (b)). The rules delay enforcement of contempt orders for ten days, which leaves time for review by the district court (Bankruptcy Rule 9020(c)). If the contemnor appeals in a timely fashion, the district court will make a de novo review (Bankruptcy Rule 9033).

There is some dispute over the power of a bankruptcy judge to exercise contempt powers in core or non-core proceedings. The general grant of power to the bankruptcy court to "issue any order, process, or judgment that is necessary or appropriate to carry out the provisions of this title" seems to support a grant of contempt powers (11 U.S.C. §105(a)). Moreover, in granting the bankruptcy judges power to hear and determine core proceedings, Congress gave the judges power to "enter appropriate orders and judgments, subject to review" of the district court, which seems to reinforce that view (28 U.S.C. §157(b)(1)).

There are doubts, however, whether Congress intended a non–Article III court to exercise contempt powers in the absence of more explicit Code language. Some courts distinguish between civil and criminal contempt orders; other courts distinguish the power to determine a contempt committed in the presence of the bankruptcy judge from the power to determine those committed elsewhere.

Even without contempt power, it seems noncontroversial that the bankruptcy court may impose sanctions on parties who violate Code provisions. Bankruptcy courts routinely impose sanctions on creditors for violations of the automatic stay and on attorneys for violations of Bankruptcy Rule 9011, which is similar to standard for sanctioning all attorneys articulated in Rule 11 of the Federal Rules of Civil Procedure.

Where to File the Bankruptcy Case

Small businesses file their bankruptcies in the federal judicial district where they are located. But big businesses have many more choices. A bankruptcy case may be commenced in the district court "in which the debtor's domicile, residence, principal place of business in the United States, or principal assets in the United States" have been for 180 days preceding filing (28 U.S.C. §1408(1)). A case also may be commenced in the district court in which an affiliate, general partner, or partnership of a business has a bankruptcy case pending (28 U.S.C. §1408(2)).

These alternative grounds for venue afford the party initiating a case — the debtor, in the overwhelming proportion of cases — a degree of choice. Businesses that are incorporated in one state, have corporate headquarters in another, and have principal operating facilities in yet another may have a number of choices. Incorporation always provides a hook for the "domicile" of a corporation, and operations in different location can be the basis for a claim of "principal place of business." If troubled affiliates are incorporated in other states or they operate in still other states, the possibilities for venue multiply.

A business cannot lock in a venue choice simply by filing in its most-favored location. Even if a filing is properly located in one jurisdiction, the court may transfer a case to another district "in the interest of justice or for the convenience of the parties" (28 U.S.C. §1412). With so many choices, it would be reasonable to assume that there are many hard-fought lawsuits over venue. Reasonable, but wrong.

In fact, if a party protests the venue choice of the business, experience shows that courts will often transfer small cases, but that they will almost never transfer a big case. Enron is a case in point. It had been incorporated in Oregon, but by the time of Enron's spectacular crash, it had 7,500 employees in Houston, including its entire management team and an extensive operations center. Another 17,500 were scattered around the globe. By contrast, there were a total of 63 employees in New York. But Enron chose a New York filing, despite the vigorous protests of Enron's employees, many Texas-based creditors, and the Texas state attorney general. The parties immediately moved to have the case transferred back to the Lone Star State, but the New York court found that it was the most convenient forum and the case stayed put.

The evidence that big companies have filed for bankruptcy in places distant from their home offices is striking. The data collected by Professor Lynn LoPucki (http://lopucki.law.ucla.edu) documents the location of the main business operations and the bankruptcy filings for all the large, publicly traded companies that have filed for bankruptcy since 1980. The data show that about two-thirds of all the billion dollar businesses in Chapter 11 have filed in a forum other than their principal place of business.

Delaware has been the big winner in the venue sweepstakes. In the early 1980s, no big cases were filed there. By the mid-1990s, Delaware had an 87 percent market share of large bankruptcy cases. By the mid-2000s, New York and Delaware together took about half of all the cases that were shopped out of other locations around the country.

Venue choice can be driven by a number of different factors. Some businesses may want to escape unhappy employees who can march around in front of the courthouse. Others may want to avoid the scrutiny of the local press, figuring it will be harder for the locals to cover proceedings in a distant locale. Others may be looking for judges who are sympathetic to debtors on specific legal issues, such as First Day Orders or extensions of exclusivity to propose a plan. Perhaps it is the expertise and efficiency of the Delaware courts that attracts big cases.[5] Or maybe the big case lawyers who are disproportionately located in New York and Delaware are calling the shots, and they prefer to stay near home and near the judges they know.

A big case bankruptcy generates lawyers' and professionals' fees, along with hotels, meals, messenger services, stenography, and enough other services that Chapter 11 is now estimated to be a $2- to $4-billion a year industry. Moreover, a big case can secure a national reputation for a bankruptcy judge. Professor LoPucki concludes that pressures on judges to make decisions that favor the people who decide where the cases will be placed forces courts into a destructive competition.

His book, *Courting Failure: How Competition for Big Cases Is Corrupting the Bankruptcy Courts* (2005) makes for lively reading. Many who disagree with the tone or some of the specific allegations in *Courting Failure* nonetheless concur that the current system of forum shopping produces powerful pressures on the judicial process. It is hard to see how any judge could be completely unmindful, if only subconsciously, that a particular decision could result in the gain or loss of millions of dollars in fees and other economic benefits for the bar and the community where that judge lives. If a ruling against management or a powerful creditor interest would have the effect of driving away the big cases and their economic benefits, a subtle but powerful pressure to avoid such a ruling seems to many observers to be inevitable.

POLICY CONSIDERATIONS

Time is a critical element in most business reorganizations. Unlike many court actions that involve disputes over liability for injuries suffered long ago, the bankruptcy case involves active monitoring of a going concern. As a result, many of the problems brought before a bankruptcy court require quick resolution. For the struggling business that cannot get a hearing on post-petition financing before payday next Friday and for the creditor that cannot get the automatic stay lifted before the business destroys the collateral, justice delayed is truly justice denied. Delay in bankruptcy proceedings has a large, substantive impact on the course of the case.

Accommodating the need for speed is particularly difficult in business bankruptcy cases because they nearly always involve a number of complex factual (and sometimes complex legal) disputes. Although lawsuits in a number of fields are growing ever more intricate, the bankruptcy case remains notable for both the variety and the number of issues and legal actions that may arise during the course of a reorganization. Again, because the case involves an ongoing business, the court may be called on to resolve issues requiring the valuation of property, the intent of parties with respect to allegedly fraudulent transactions occurring years earlier, the advisability of long-term financing proposals, the necessity of termination of employee health insurance plans, and so on. Not only are the issues diverse, but the parties that come forward to litigate them may change from issue to issue. Alliances among parties may form, break up, and re-form as parties see potential gain or loss in proposed resolutions of different disputes.

In all bankruptcy cases there is acute awareness that money spent wrangling over the rights of the parties is not money spent to move the business toward a successful reorganization or money distributed to the creditors. Many observers believe that some portion of the businesses that fail in Chapter 11 do so because resources that were essential to the reorganization were dissipated in litigation. Other observers note that estates often consume enormous resources that would have gone to the creditors in an early liquidation. In both instances, the value-enhancement norms of the Code are directly implicated in the practices and procedures used in bankruptcy cases.

Once again, the Code's value-enhancement norms become intertwined with its distributional values. To the extent that a party has the power to delay proceedings or otherwise to derail a pending reorganization or liquidation, that party can negotiate for better treatment in return for not holding up the works. The ability to delay proceedings when there is no underlying legal basis for any claim has been blamed, for example, for payments being made to shareholders in publicly traded corporations in plan confirmations (so-called "hostage payments" to reflect their origin not in law, but in the power to hold up the progress of the case).[6] Because of the need to negotiate multiparty settlements that can break apart in an instant and because of the premium on consensual plans, bankruptcy is an area particularly susceptible to the influence of holdout positions. Procedural rules or jurisdictional maneuvering may be used to squeeze a better deal for a negotiating party, thereby implicating the distributive norms of the bankruptcy scheme.

In part to control the costs of reorganization and to prevent the dissipation of assets, the Code gives the courts not only the power to make summary dispositions of creditor actions, but also sweeping powers to monitor the business's expenses directly. One of the most notable is the court's power to monitor the business's legal expenses. The business can engage counsel only with the approval of the court, and it can pay its legal bills only if the court approves such payments (11 U.S.C. §§327(a), 328). The court can review the attorney's bills at any level of specificity, from cutting back on photocopying to refusing reimbursement for counsel's hourly charges. Many courts review fees *sua sponte*, noting that the Code requires approval from the court (and hence an independent inquiry) before such fees can be paid, even if no creditor objects to the attorney's request for payment from the estate. Similarly, the court also monitors any expenditures by the business for employment of any other professionals or experts (11 U.S.C. §§327, 328). Even with such extraordinary power vested in the bankruptcy courts to review the expenses of the business, there is a growing sense that administrative expenses, particularly attorneys' fees, consume an excessive portion of the business's assets in a reorganization effort.

The practical realities that inhere in the resolution of a bankruptcy case shape the policy issues that arise in determining bankruptcy jurisdiction and procedure. The statute and the courts are necessarily concerned with finding an appropriate balance between protecting the rights of parties to air their disputes and maintaining procedures that do not themselves reduce the value of the estate. Concerns over the time, complexity, and resource consumption in parties' maneuvering in bankruptcy hover at the edge of every bankruptcy case and have a very real impact on the resources ultimately distributed to the creditors.

CROSS-BORDER BANKRUPTCIES

Law follows reality. In the business world, companies are no longer confined by national boundaries. Many companies hold assets, do business and otherwise conduct their affairs across borders. When those companies get into financial trouble, the question of how — and where — to deal with the outstanding obligations becomes hotly contested.

With the adoption of the modern Bankruptcy Code in 1978, the United States added an innovation that would permit U.S. bankruptcy courts to cooperate with home country bankruptcy courts abroad (11 U.S.C. §§303(b)(4), 304–306). This was a unilateral initiative, requiring no reciprocity. Early efforts were tentative, and, for many years, other jurisdictions did not reciprocate. So, for example, when a U.S. company filed for bankruptcy, creditors around the globe often persuaded local courts to permit them to seize assets located in those distant ports. Despite the broad language of the bankruptcy code to reach assets "wherever located," as a practical matter the U.S. bankruptcy affected only assets in the United States. Creditors in the rest of the world grabbed what they could.

Over time, however, other courts began to respond to this initiative and to a growing belief in international financial circles that a more coordinated solution to multinational bankruptcy should be found. The idea emerged, pushed along with considerable grace and perseverance by Professor Jay Westbrook, that a bankruptcy filing located in one country should determine the procedures and the substantive rules for the reorganization or liquidation of the business.[7] Courts in other countries should follow the lead of the home country court. By substituting some form of cooperation for the grab rule, more businesses could survive and ultimately pay more to all the creditors.

The change in attitudes was reflected in the United Nations' promulgation in 1997 of a Model Law of Cross-Border Insolvency for international cooperation in bankruptcy matters. The United States was a very active participant in the development of the Model Law. The 2005 amendments to the bankruptcy code included a new Chapter 15, which was the U.S. adoption of the Model Law provisions.

With the adoption of Chapter 15, the United States made yet another public declaration of its support for international cooperation of cross-border insolvencies. The U.S. courts were officially declared open to provide assistance to courts administering bankruptcies elsewhere in the world. By filing a Chapter 15, a party from a foreign bankruptcy may start down a path to exercise dominion over property of the bankruptcy business that is located in the United States.

But Chapter 15 was not intended to initiate a great change is U.S. law. Section 304, particularly as interpreted by the courts, had already pushed toward cooperation. Even so, there are differences. Before Chapter 15 was enacted, the Code seemed to say that the U.S. bankruptcy courts would cooperate only when the provisions of the other law were not different in any way that would adversely affect some U.S. creditor. That rule would mean, of course, that we would rarely cooperate. On the other hand, the earlier rule was also interpreted as requiring only a general similarity to our law, a similarity that may be found in the laws of a number of other countries. Faced with the conflicting policy goals of international cooperation and protection of U.S. creditors, Congress simply incorporated both. For example, U.S. courts had struggled with the contradictions inherent in Section 304 when security interests or other alleged interests in property were at issue because Section 304 created a mechanism for cooperation at the same time that it required protection of U.S. creditors in language much more specific than that of Section 1522, which is clearly designed to give the courts more discretion in the context of a mandate to cooperate (11 U.S.C. §§304(c), 1522, 1525–1527). The courts were left to work it out.

Chapter 15 retains the common law approach of using an ancillary proceeding as the vehicle of cooperation, but it also permits multiple bankruptcies to proceed on parallel tracks in different countries. The U.S. courts are instructed to cooperate with foreign "main" proceedings, which are proceedings in the country where the "center of main interests" of the business is located, a test taken from the European Union Regulation (11 U.S.C. §§101(23), 1502(4)). A "foreign representative" (11 U.S.C. §101(24)) may file for recognition of a foreign proceeding in the United States under Section 1515 and recognition will be granted quickly in most cases using various presumptions (11 U.S.C. §§1515–1517). Upon recognition, the automatic stay goes into effect with the same force and same limitations as under domestic bankruptcy law and the court is given broad powers, including the grant of additional injunctive relief, the use of U.S. discovery tools, and the turnover of assets within its control to the foreign representative, who is also empowered to operate the business (11 U.S.C. §§1520(a)(3), 1521(a)-(b)). Foreign nonmain proceedings (that is, proceedings in countries other than the "main" one) are granted only quite limited recognition and cooperation (11 U.S.C. §1521(c)). The foreign representative is required to make full disclosure to the United States bankruptcy court of the status of proceedings elsewhere in the world and to keep that information up to date.

The process of negotiation requires the inclusion of provisions that give some primacy to local parallel proceedings (called "concurrent" proceedings" in Section 1529), but the legislative history and the amendment to Section 305 make it clear that the court has broad discretion to dismiss the local U.S. case in favor of an ancillary approach in deference to the foreign proceeding where it is pending in the home country of the debtor. Some commentators have argued that the venue abuses that have occurred on a national scale will begin to repeat themselves in the international arena.

Perhaps the most far-reaching change in the Model Law, in the United States and elsewhere, is the adoption of provisions expressly encouraging direct communication between courts in multinational bankruptcy cases (11 U.S.C. §§1525–1526). These sections also authorize direct communication between courts and bankruptcy trustees. In both situations, appropriate notice and supervision are also required. These provisions are not merely optimistic visions. Even before Chapter 15 was adopted, in a case in which the United Kingdom and the United States had gotten at cross purposes, a transatlantic telephone call between a British judge and an American judge enabled the courts and parties to avoid an unpleasant and costly conflict between these generally friendly court systems.[8] The idea of judges talking directly to each other was a little shocking, but the American Law Institute helped pave the way with its transnational insolvency report that strongly endorsed such communications, providing a set of guidelines for courts and lawyers to use.[9] The Canadian-based International Insolvency Institute has translated the ALI Guidelines into a number of languages for use all over the world.

Adoption of Chapter 15 has expanded the use of bankruptcies to solve cross-border economic problems, but the U.S. initiatives are not the only ones. A number of international institutions — notably the International Monetary Fund and the World Bank — have gotten interested in reform of bankruptcy laws, both domestic and international. Law reform organizations have also developed projects in international bankruptcy cooperation.

The United Nations has also been active in transnational insolvencies. In fact, it moved before the United States did, establishing a Model Law on Cross-Border Insolvencies promulgated by the United Nations Commission on International Trade Law (UNCITRAL). Unlike a treaty or convention, a model law is offered for adoption by each country in the hope that its adoption by a number of countries will begin the process of cooperation and, eventually, harmonization. As noted above, the UN's Model Law furnished the guide for the provisions in Chapter 15 in the U.S. Bankruptcy Code.

The Transnational Insolvency Project of the American Law Institute was also mentioned earlier. Its purpose is to go the next step beyond the U.N.'s Model Law to improve cooperation among the three NAFTA countries, Canada, Mexico, and the United States, in multinational insolvencies. The project has produced authoritative summaries of the bankruptcy laws of each of the three countries and a statement of Principles of Cooperation. At the heart of the ALI Principles is the idea of a global perspective. Each principle is designed to encourage the courts and the parties to look at such cases overall, seeking the best results for the parties regardless of local advantage.

Finally, in 2002, the European Union adopted a bankruptcy "regulation," which is a law that is binding on all EU member countries and enforceable in their courts. Over time experts anticipate that the law will tend to improve cooperation and coordination in trans-EU cases, although it does not go as far in the cosmopolitan direction as many observers had hoped. Its most important feature may simply be the fact that it is an EU regulation and therefore will be subject to uniform interpretation through the European Court of Justice. With this mechanism in place, the EU regulations will offer the first example of a truly international bankruptcy regime.

CONCLUSION

The 1978 Code was designed to rationalize the jurisdictional rules and to provide a fair, efficient system for administering bankruptcy estates. The changes were designed to focus the bankruptcy process on speedy liquidation or reorganization, rather than have time and assets wasted on jurisdictional and procedural disputes. The bankruptcy courts were given more independent status, and the role of the bankruptcy judges was reshaped to make it similar to the role of other trial court judges. The subsequent constitutional and political disputes and the resulting 1984 amendments have produced a more complex structure. Even so, the grant of jurisdictional power to the district courts and through them to the bankruptcy courts is broad, and the bankruptcy courts resolve, subject to review, the bulk of the issues that arise in bankruptcy cases.

The bankruptcy system still has a number of important unresolved procedural and jurisdictional issues. The most critical question is whether the jurisdictional system is constitutionally sound. A number of other subsidiary questions persist as well, including those concerning jury trials, contempt orders, and distinctions among kinds of bankruptcy proceedings. Forum selection in big cases has produced a bifurcated business bankruptcy system in which only a handful of courts handle billion-dollar cases, while all other courts never see a large case.

With the advent of multinational companies filing for bankruptcy both in the United States and abroad, each aspect of the Chapter 11 system will be tested and re-tested against competing models in other nations. Operations could change dramatically if Congress or the courts make an unexpected move to alter the current balances. In the meantime, as befits any system built on practical realities, the bankruptcy system functions without full resolution of these questions, pushing cases forward day by day.

Endnotes

CHAPTER 1

1. Robert Lawless & Elizabeth Warren, *The Myth of the Disappearing Business Bankruptcy*, 93 Cal. L. Rev. 745 (2005), reprinted in 47 Corporate Practice Commentator 593 (2005).

2. Elizabeth Warren & Jay Lawrence Westbrook, The Success of Chapter 11: A Challenge to the Critics, _____ U. Mich. L. Rev. _____ (2009 forthcoming).

3. U.S. Const. art. I, § 8.

4. Elizabeth Warren, *The Untenable Case for Repeal of Chapter 11*, 102 Yale L.J. 437, 452–455 (1992).

5. Thomas H. Jackson, *The Logic and Limits of Bankruptcy Law* (1986); Douglas Baird, *The Uneasy Case for Corporate Reorganization*, 15 J. Legal Studies 127 (1986).

6. Douglas Baird, *Loss Distribution, Forum Shopping, and Bankruptcy: A Reply to Warren*, 54 U. Chi. L. Rev. 815 (1987).

7. Elizabeth Warren, *Bankruptcy Policymaking in an Imperfect World*, 92 U. Mich. L. Rev. 336 (1993)

8. Arturo Bris, Ivo Welch, & Ning Zhu, "The Costs of Bankruptcy: Chapter 7 Liquidation vs. Chapter 11 Reorganization," at 6 (August 24, 2005) (study of 225 Chapter 11 corporate cases and 61 Chapter 7 corporate cases from Arizona and New York filed from 1995 to 2001) (manuscript on file with author). In a review of what they describe as a "similar" dataset, Professors Baird, Bris, and Zhu add the caveat that cases under $200,000 pay little to the general unsecured creditors, and that payments tend to come only from companies with larger assets. That analysis is based on a study of 17 small cases from a sample of 139 cases filed in Arizona and New York. Douglas Baird, Arturo Bris, & Ning Zhu, "The Dynamics of Large and Small Chapter 11 Cases: An Empirical Study" (December 2005) (manuscript on file with author).

9. Ed Flynn, *Administrative Office of the U.S. Courts, Statistical Analysis of Chapter 11*, at 10–11 (1989).

10. The Brookings Study did not focus on the proportion of cases that confirmed a plan. Instead, it found that two years after their Chapter XI proceedings were closed, approximately one-third of the debtors were still operating their own

businesses. But they had eliminated the cases that closed before confirmation, so direct comparison among studies is not possible. David Stanley & Marjorie Girth, *Bankruptcy: Problem, Process, Reform* 109, 115, 143, Table 7-8 (1971).

11. An earlier report by Professor Lynn LoPucki reported a somewhat higher confirmation rate (27 percent), but the data were all collected from one district in Missouri and only 57 cases were studied, so that the much larger, much better-funded GAO study continued to dominate the conventional wisdom. Moreover, the other criticisms launched in the article hardly served as an advertisement for success in Chapter 11. Lynn LoPucki, *Debtor in Full Control: Systems Failure under Chapter 11 of the Bankruptcy Code* (Part 1), 57 Am. Bankr. L.J. 99 (1983).

12. Warren & Westbrook, *supra* note 2.

13. *Id.*

14. *Id.*

15. Lynn M. LoPucki & Joseph W. Doherty, *The Determinants of Professional Fees in Large Bankruptcy Reorganization Cases*, 1 J. Empirical L. Stud. 111, 140 (2004).

16. Stephen Lubben, *The Direct Costs of Corporate Reorganization: An Empirical Examination of Professional Fees in Large Chapter 11 Cases*, 74 Am. Bankr. L.J. 509, 515 (2000).

17. Brian Betker, *The Administrative Costs of Debt Restructuring: Some Recent Evidence*, 26 Financial Management 56 (1999).

18. Robert M. Lawless, Stephen P. Ferris, Narayanan Jayaraman, & Anil K. Makhija, *A Glimpse at Professional Fees and Other Direct Costs in Small Firm Bankruptcies*, 1994 U. Ill. L. Rev. 847, 868; Stephen P. Ferris & Robert M. Lawless, *The Expenses of Financial Distress: The Direct Costs of Chapter 11*, 31 U. Pitt. L. Rev. (1999).

19. Stuart Gilson, *Transactions Costs and Capital Structure Choice: Evidence from Financially Distressed Firms*, 52 Journal of Finance 161; Stuart Gilson, John Kose, & Larry Lang, *Troubled Debt Restructurings: An Empirical Study of Private Reorganization of Firms in Default*, 27 J. Fin. Econ. 315 (1990).

CHAPTER 2

1. There was speculation in the early 1980s that the proportion of involuntary petitions might rise, especially as more and more lawyers who were not specialists became familiar with the enormous power of bankruptcy law, in particular the power to defeat security interests and other transactions. In a study of involuntary petitions, however, Professor Susan Block-Lieb explained that the proportion of involuntary petitions has remained low — and argued that it should continue to do so. Susan Block-Lieb, *Why Creditors File So Few Involuntary Petitions and Why the Number Is Not Too Small*, 57 Brook. L. Rev. 803 (1991). Block-Lieb discusses competing bankruptcy policy goals, including a desire to encourage non-bankruptcy workouts that is in tension in some respects with the desire to encourage creditors to file earlier while a debtor still has value, which she claims are fostered by the complexity of the involuntary procedures.

2. Lynn LoPucki & William Whitford, *Bargaining over Equity's Share in the Bankruptcy Reorganizations of Large, Publicly Held Companies*, 139 Penn. L. Rev.

125 (1990). See also Gilson, *Management Turnover and Financial Distress*, 25 J. Fin. Econ. 241 (1989).

3. Lynn LoPucki, *The Debtor in Full Control: Systems Failure under Chapter 11 of the Bankruptcy Code?*, 57 Am. Bankr. L.J. 247, 263–266 (1983).

4. Setoffs against commodity and security contracts in margin accounts and setoffs by repo participants have some limited protection (11 U.S.C. § 362(b)(6),(7)). The Secretary of Housing and Urban Development may foreclose a mortgage insured under the National Housing Act for multiple-unit housing (11 U.S.C. § 362(b)(8)). Taxing authorities may issue tax delinquency notices (11 USC 362(b)(9)). And special provisions exist for actions brought by the Secretary of Transportation under the Ship Mortgage Act (11 U.S.C. § 362(b)(12), (13)).

5. 484 U.S. 365 (1985).

6. For more information on SAREs, see Kenneth N. Klee, *One Size Fits Some: Single Asset Real Estate Bankruptcy Cases*, 87 Cornell L. Rev. 1285 (2002).

7. But even here, the Code strives for balance. The estate can use rents to make adequate protection payments, while mortgage lenders can insist on an interest rate set at the preexisting contract rate, which helps the mortgage lender in the typical falling market.

8. See American Bankruptcy Institute, *Perception and Reality: American Bankruptcy Institute Survey on Selected Provisions of the 1984 Amendments to the Bankruptcy Code* 45–46 (1987).

9. *See, e.g., In re Braniff Airways, Inc.*, 700 F.2d 935 (5th Cir. 1983).

10. This point was clarified in *United States v. Whiting Pools, Inc.* 462 U.S. 198 (1983). The IRS had seized the debtor's assets pre-petition. The debtor had no right to recover them without paying the taxes due. The estate, however, had a possessory interest under Section 542(a). This, said the Supreme Court, required the return of the collateral to the estate, with appropriate provisions made for affording the IRS adequate protection.

11. 469 U.S. 274 (1985).

12. The interim management of the bankruptcy estate is discussed in the next chapter.

CHAPTER 3

1. Jay Lawrence Westbrook, *The Control of Wealth in Bankruptcy*, 82 Tex. L. Rev. 795 (2004).

2. Douglas G. Baird & Robert K. Rasmussen, *The End of Bankruptcy*, 55 Stan. L. Rev. 751 (2002). Others have commented on the increasing power of secured creditors in business bankruptcies. Elizabeth Warren & Jay L. Westbrook, *Secured Parties in Possession*, 22 Am. Bankr. Inst. J., 12 (2003).

3. Lynn LoPucki & William Whitford, *Corporate Governance in the Bankruptcy Reorganization of Large, Publicly Traded Companies*, 141 U. Pa. L. Rev. 669, 729 (1991).

4. Brian Betker, *Management's Incentives, Equity's Bargaining Power, and Deviations from Absolute Priority in Chapter 11 Bankruptcies*, 68 J. Bus. 161 (1995).

5. Stuart C. Gilson, *Management Turnover and Financial Distress*, J. Fin. Econ. 241 (1989).

6. Lynn LoPucki, *The Debtor in Full Control — Systems Failure under Chapter 11 of the Bankruptcy Code?*, 57 Am. Bankr. L.J. 247, 266–69 (1983).

7. For a discussion of the implications of high management turnover rates and the effect on the decision to file bankruptcy, *see* Elizabeth Warren, *The Untenable Case for Repeal of Chapter 11*, 102 Yale L.J. 437 (1993), *reprinted in* Charles J. Tabb, *Bankruptcy Anthology* (2002).

CHAPTER 4

1. Vern Countryman, *Executory Contracts in Bankruptcy: Part I*, 57 Minn. L. Rev. 439 (1973); *Part II*, 58 Minn. L. Rev. 479 (1974).

2. Jay Lawrence Westbrook, *A Functional Analysis of Executory Contracts*, 74 Minn. L. Rev. 227, 228 (1989).

3. For a discussion of the cases in which no money damages can substitute for an equitable remedy and the court permits the equitable remedy to survive bankruptcy, *see* Lynn LoPucki & Christopher Mirick, *Strategies for Creditors in Bankruptcy Proceedings* 103–04 § 2.17 (5th Ed. 2006) (citing cases).

4. Oliver Wendell Holmes, *The Common Law* 236 (Mark DeWolfe Howe ed., 1961).

5. *See, e.g.*, William Fletcher, *Fletcher Cyclopedia of the Law of Private Corporations* § 8219 (rev. perm. ed. 1962).

6. *See, e.g.*, Harry Henn, *Law of Corporations* § 231 (2d ed. 1970).

7. Adam Levitin, *Towards a Federal Common Law of Bankruptcy: Judicial Lawmaking in a Statutory Regime*, 80 Am. Bankr. L. J. 1 (2006).

CHAPTER 5

1. Elizabeth Warren & Jay Lawrence Westbrook, The Success of Chapter 11: A Challenge to the Critics, _____ U. Mich. L. Rev. _____ (2009 forthcoming).

2. Lynn LoPucki & William Whitford, *Venue Choice*, 1991 Wis. L. Rev. 11, 138–41. In small cases, only a few creditors may take the trouble to vote on a plan. The consent of the creditors in such cases is obviously more attenuated, perhaps meaning only that they did not object enough to record a negative vote. *See* Lynn LoPucki, *The Debtor in Full Control — Systems Failure under Chapter 11 of the Bankruptcy Code?*, 57 Am. Bankr. L.J. 247, 266–69 (1983).

3. Elizabeth Warren & Jay Lawrence Westbrook, *Financial Characteristics of Businesses in Bankruptcy*, 73 Am. Bankr. L.J. 499, 538, table 8 (1999).

4. *Id.* at 529, Figure 3.

5. The figure in the 2005 amendments was $2,000,000, but it is subject to inflation adjustments every three years. The number listed here will change again in March 2010.

6. *See* Report of the National Bankruptcy Review Commission, Chapter 5: Individual Commissioner Views, Dissent of the Honorable Edith Jones and Commissioner James I. Shepard (1997).

7. *See* Report of the National Bankruptcy Review Commission, Chapter 2: Small Business Proposals 2.5.1 (1997).

8. *See, e.g.,* William Fletcher, *Fletcher Cyclopedia of the Law of Private Corporations* § 8219 (rev. perm. ed. 1962).

9. For a penetrating discussion of SAREs in bankruptcy, *see* Kenneth N. Klee, *One Size Fits Some: Single Asset Real Estate Bankruptcy Cases,* 87 Cornell L. Rev. 1285 (2002).

10. 526 U.S. 434 (1999).

11. The tax treatment of such a move would undoubtedly be tangled. Debt forgiveness in bankruptcy enjoys some tax relief, but permanent injunctions may not receive such favored treatment. Internal Revenue Code § 108(e).

1. U.S. Const. art. I, § 8.

2. 458 U.S. 50 (1982).

3. 458 U.S. at 71.

4. U.S. Const. amend. VII.

5. *See, e.g.,* Marcus Cole, *"Delaware Is Not a State": Are We Witnessing Jurisdictional Competition in Bankruptcy?,* 55 Vand. L. Rev. 1845 (2002).

6. *E.g.,* Lynn LoPucki & William Whitford, *Bargaining Over Equity's Share in the Bankruptcy Reorganization of Large, Publicly Held Companies,* 139 U. Pa. L. Rev. 125, 145–57 (1990).

7. *E.g.,* Jay Lawrence Westbrook, *International Judicial Negotiation,* 38 Tex. Int'l L.J. 567 (2003).

8. *In re Cenargo Int'l, Plc,* 294 B.R. 571 (Bankr. S.D.N.Y. 2003).

9. ALI Principles of Cooperation among the NAFTA Countries Proc. Prin. 10, 57 and App. B (2003).

Glossary

ABC. Assignment for the benefit of creditors involves transferring property to a trustee for distribution to creditors without filing for bankruptcy.

Absolute priority rule. When a business is liquidated, the assets must be paid out first to creditors and then, only if creditors have been paid in full, to equity holders.

Adequate protection. In bankruptcy, if a secured creditor asks the court to lift the automatic stay so that it can reach collateral held by the debtor, a court will grant the stay unless the creditor is "adequately protected." A court will usually find the secured creditor is adequately protected only if there is excess collateral above the loan value, there is small risk that the collateral may decline in risk, or the debtor offers payments or additional security to ensure that the creditor's interest in collateral is protected while the bankruptcy is pending.

Appeals, bankruptcy. A losing party may appeal from a bankruptcy court order to the district court where the case is heard, and then to a circuit court, the court of appeals, and the Supreme Court. Alternatively, if all parties consent and the parties are in a BAP jurisdiction, an appeal may go from the bankruptcy court to a Bankruptcy Appellate Panel, to a circuit court and the Supreme Court.

Automatic stay. When a debtor files for bankruptcy, with only a few exceptions, all attempts to collect from the debtor, from the debtor's property or from the newly formed bankruptcy estate are halted by operation of law.

Balance sheet. Assets are equal to liabilities plus equity; the balance sheet gives the details of this formula for a business.

Bankruptcy appellate panel. An alternative forum for hearing appeals from a bankruptcy court, staffed by bankruptcy judges from the circuit, available only if both parties consent, often called a BAP.

Bankruptcy estate. A legal entity created automatically when a petition in bankruptcy is filed; after filing, the estate is the owner of all the debtor's property.

Best Interests Test. Each creditor in Chapter 11 or Chapter 13 is entitled under the plan to received payments over time that are at least the present value of the amount that creditor would have received in a liquidation.

Bona fide purchaser. A good faith purchaser for value, not someone who was a party to fraud or who was the recipient of a gift.

Collateral. Property that is subject to a security interest; if the debtor cannot repay an obligation, the creditor with an interest in collateral may turn to that collateral for satisfaction of the debt.

Collective rights. The rights enjoyed by creditors as a group, rather than their individual rights.

Constructive fraud. Fraud inferred from the facts rather than from the intent of the parties.

Core proceedings. Core proceedings, which are undefined in the bankruptcy code, may be heard by bankruptcy judges, while non-core proceedings must be heard by district courts; examples of core proceedings include allowance of claims, objections to discharge, and all bankruptcy administrative matters.

Cramdown. Approving a Chapter 11 plan over the objection of a class of creditors.

Creditor. The entity owed a debt.

Cross-border bankruptcies. The bankruptcy of a business with assets in two or more countries.

Earmark. To identify that money to be lent to a debtor will be used to pay off another specific debt.

Equitable ownership. Owner of the beneficial interest, as opposed to the bare legal title.

Equitable subordination. A creditor's demotion in the order of payment because the creditor engaged in conduct injurious to the other creditors or the creditor exercised power typically reserved to owners.

Executory contract. A contract that has performance outstanding on both sides.

Feasibility. The judgment a court must make about whether a Chapter 11 plan is likely to succeed.

First Day Orders. The orders a bankruptcy court issues very early in the case (usually the first day), often undertaken to keep the business running immediately after a bankruptcy filing.

Fraudulent conveyance. A transfer that was undertaken with intent to hinder, delay, or defraud creditors, or that was undertaken while the debtor was insolvent and was for less than reasonably equivalent value.

Fraudulent transfer. Same as fraudulent conveyance.

Going concern. The value of an operational business that exceeds the value of the individual assets.

Injunction. An order from a court to prevent an action.

Insider. A person or entity with one of certain close relationships with the debtor.

Involuntary petition. The petition that creditors file with the court to have a business declared bankrupt.

Ipso facto. Refers to provisions in a contract that trigger automatically to terminate the contract when the debtor is in financial trouble.

Judgment lien. A lien against property created by state process (usually a sheriff, but sometimes through filing) against the property in order to enforce the order of a court.

Judgment lien creditor. A creditor that obtained a judgment from a court that an amount was due and executed on that judgment through state process.

Jury trials. Permissible in a bankruptcy court only if both parties consent.

Lien. Security interest (if voluntary) or statutory lien (if created by operation of law).

Leveraged buyouts. Financing the purchase of a business by taking a security interest in the assets of the business that is the target of the sale in order to secure the loan for the purchase price.

Liquidation. Sale of all the assets of a business and distribution of the value to the creditors and, if they have been paid in full, the shareholders.

Oversecured. Sufficient collateral to exceed the outstanding loan.

Perfection. An action taken at state law, such as filing or possession, that makes a security interest enforceable against other parties, including a trustee in bankruptcy.

Plan confirmation. A court order that a proposed plan of reorganization has been confirmed and will control the legal rights of the parties.

Pre-packaged plans. Chapter 11 plans for which the plan proponents began soliciting votes for the plan before the bankruptcy was filed.

Present value dollar. The value of a dollar paid immediately, which contrasts with the discounted value of a dollar paid in the future (see time value of money).

Proceedings, core, non-core. Core proceedings, which are undefined in the bankruptcy code, may be heard by bankruptcy judges, while non-core proceedings must be heard by district courts; examples of core proceedings include allowance of claims, objections to discharge, and all bankruptcy administrative matters.

Purchase Money Security Interests. When a creditor lends the money necessary to purchase the item used as collateral or when the creditor is the seller of the item, the resulting security interest is a purchase money security interest (sometimes known as a PMSI).

Reasonably equivalent value. An exchange on roughly equivalent terms; if there is no REV and the debtor is insolvent, creditors may have the right to set aside the transaction.

Reclamation. Rights given to sellers of goods to recover those goods if they were delivered shortly before bankruptcy.

Recourse/non-recourse. A loan is recourse when the debtor is liable on the loan; it is non-recourse if the creditor can reach collateral but is unable to enforce any obligation against the debtor personally.

Reorganization. Usually refers to the development and adoption of a plan to deal with a business's outstanding debts in Chapter 11.

SARE. A single asset real estate case.

Secured. A creditor with an interest in a particular piece of collateral to be used to satisfy the loan if the debtor is unable to do so.

Single asset real estate. A business that is almost exclusively about the use of a price of real estate, such as the operation of an apartment or office building.

Small business debtor. A debtor with debts of less than $2.19 million will be subject to special rules in bankruptcy.

Statutory liens. Liens against property that operate by state law rather than by consent of the parties.

Strong-arm. The term that refers to the power a TIB has to terminate the rights of an unperfected secured creditor in any collateral.

Stay litigation. A dispute in court over the application of the automatic stay.

Time value of money. Recognition that receiving money today so that it can be invested is more valuable than receiving the same number of dollars in the future.

Turnover. A court order that requires a party to give a piece of property to the entity to whom the court directs.

Undersecured. A creditor with an enforceable security interest in collateral that is worth less that the outstanding debt.

Unrecorded. When a creditor has a written security interest, but the creditor fails to perfect its interest by filing, the interest is often referred to as unrecorded.

Unsecured. A general creditor that has no enforceable interest in any specific item of property belonging to the debtor.

Venue. The district in which a bankruptcy case is heard.

Voidable preference. A transfer of an interest of the debtor, made within 90 days of bankruptcy (1 year for insiders) while the debtor was insolvent, to or for the benefit of a creditor that would permit the creditor to get more than the creditor would have gotten in liquidation without the transfer.

Voluntary petition. Nearly all bankruptcies begin with petitions filed voluntarily by the debtor; a few begin when the creditors file a petition to force the debtor into bankruptcy.

Voting. In Chapter 11 cases, creditors whose interests will be impaired by the plan, can vote yes or no on adoption of the plan.

Workout. A voluntary agreement by which parties my agree to readjust their debt obligations.

Index

210 *Index*